- You are new to business networking and want down to earth, fast-track advice on what to expect

- You want to network but keep putting it off because you dread the thought of going into a room full of strangers

- You fear public speaking and want to learn how to give a brilliant 60 second pitch

- You want to develop the skill of how to talk about your business with confidence

- You want to take the pressure off yourself when you network

- You want to learn how to strike instant and lasting rapport that will lead the way to ongoing repeated business

- You want to use social media to augment your real life networking activity

- You are looking for a way to enhance your word of mouth publicity

How to Network Your Way to Success

by Paul Ryan

Dedication

To my wife, my children and all those who helped me Network My Way to Success

Acknowledgements

"It is literally true that you can succeed best and quickest by helping others to succeed." – Napoleon Hill

With that classic quote in mind I would like to thank the following people who have gone out of their way to help me succeed in getting this book from a distant goal to an immediate reality.

Thanks to Mark Collingwood, Beth Parmar, Alex Bourne, Richard Abrahams, Peter Cannon, Michael Nagles, Heather Phoenix, Viki Brockett, Adam Hollier and all the contributors who appear throughout this book. Thanks also to Jeanette Lendon for the head shot on the back cover.

Everybody has given of their time and expertise wholeheartedly and without expectation of gaining anything in return for their generosity. This list of people represents how networking really does work in so many ways and on so many different levels.

I feel I have to give special mention to Dee Blick, author of The Ultimate Guide to Writing and Marketing a Bestselling Book – on a Shoestring Budget. She has given me incredible tutelage, encouragement and guidance. I hope I make the bestseller list as a testament to you, your kindness and your commitment to all those who have a book inside them.

Thank you one and all.

Contents

Part One

Networking and me – Networking and you

Chapter 6 p62

How to handle your 60 second pitch

- Learn a simple but highly effective piece of body language that will enhance the way you feel before and during your pitch
- Learn the 6o second ABC
- How to structure your pitch

Chapter 7 p71

Five more great tips on how to handle your 60 second pitch

- Further invaluable augmentation of your skills as a public speaker

Chapter 8 p81

After the pitch is over

- How to best capitalise on your networking meetings
- The value of the follow up
- How to be remembered

Part Two
Networking Know-how

- Learn to move forward with courage and determination
- Discover all that is wrong with your comfort zone and why it will do anything it can to stop you networking!

- The best way to double your networking capabilities
- The value of accountability

- Creating a business card to be proud of
- Getting the best out of your card
- What to do with the information on a business card to make it work to your advantage

Chapter 12   p134

The meaning and value of help

- How to fast track your ability to deepen your relationships with your fellow networkers
- Why helping others is the best way to help yourself
- How to enhance the feel good factor of networking

Part Three

Networking Online – Networking In Life

Chapter 13   p141

What is the best networking group for you?

- BNI vs 4Networking
- An insight into the two largest business networking groups in the country and which one may best suit you

Chapter 14   p161

What is the best networking group for you?
The Sequel

- Non-subscription groups and independents
- A round-up of the more intimate and bespoke groups that you can chose from

About Paul Ryan

Paul's background is placed firmly in the theatre. He was a child actor performing in the West End at the tender age of 13 back in 1978. He has appeared in over 65 theatre productions, 30 or so commercials and a smattering of TV shows.

As a second string to his bow Paul moved into the world of corporate training and in 2012 he set up his own business, Improve On You which he promptly failed to make work until he started networking.
Since that time Paul has developed Improve On You workshops in presentation skills, confidence building and open communication and has taken those into small businesses and international corporations.

Paul is also a lively and amusing public speaker making regular appearances at conferences and networking events.

This is Paul's first book.

Foreword

by Mark Bowden, communication trainer to Fortune 500 and G8 leaders.

No one is ever successful alone!
Anyone who ever achieves success does it with the help of a team.

I don't care how smart you are, how great your ideas may be or how effective you are at what you do: if you are not part of a group who trust each other and work together in supporting each other's goals, then your initiatives are doomed!

That's why if you are not actively surrounding yourself and your business with a team of customers, clients, suppliers and partners who know you, like you, trust you and want you to thrive – then your chances of success are unfortunately less than slight.

So it's your primary job as a business owner to work at building a supportive community around your product or service and to actively support others within that community too. In this way you are working to build a healthy ecosystem that supplies the resources for everyone to flourish. This community is what we call your 'network'.
As a successful entrepreneur you have to build this network. You have to build it fast to first get established, and you have to build it smart to compete and survive the changes within your market and ultimately to win a prime position.
So how are you going to do all of that?

Here's how you'll best start...

Reading this book, you're going to get help today from a real expert in building a business network: someone who has a world-class background in communication; someone who has taken the rocky and less travelled road in establishing a successful business for himself; someone who has created and continues to build a strong network around him that know him, like him, and trust his talents, skills and experience in teaching the strategies, tools and techniques that can help anyone improve their impact when networking.

Paul Ryan is here to improve on you and accelerate your impact when networking. Follow Paul's story and learn the tools and techniques he has used and developed along his journey to success and apply them to yours!

You'll find this book friendly, entertaining, interesting, insightful and ultimately helpful – just like Paul himself! His observations on the barriers to building your network and how to overcome them with real impact will help you walk into any room confident in your abilities to make networking work for you and your business.

Paul is a force of nature in everything he does. I have admired him and learned from him as a performer just as I now admire him as an expert and master trainer in networking. So read this book, take its advice, use its wisdom and actions and reap the advantage of instantly improving on your business success.

www.truthplane.com

Part One

Networking and me – Networking and you

Before we go any further, I want to start this book at the end.

The End

There. Good, wasn't it! Money well spent – a thoughtful, concise look at the current trend in business networking. How it works, how to make it work for you and how we all benefit from making it work for each other.

It was a book that was funny, full of great advice and stuffed with brilliant tips and techniques to help you take the nerves out of walking into a room full of strangers and giving your 60 second pitch. The result? The room full of strangers eventually turns into a room full of friends, all willing to go out of their way to help, advise and recommend you to others that they know in the business community so that you get work and, most importantly; though it's terribly un-British to say it:

Make Money!

(There, I said it, and I'm British)

Added to that, this book was glistening with humorous anecdotes, dripping with helpful insights and positively sodden with good advice. It also worked as a guide to all the various types of networking groups that you will come across out there, written in the hope that, as you start on your journey into the strange and exotic world of networking, you will go in forewarned and therefore forearmed.

The reason why I am starting this book at the end is because that is precisely where I am at the time of writing. I stand at the end only my second year as a committed networker. Yes, that's right and that's all; 24 short months and all of a sudden I'm an expert on the subject! Only three months into my own networking experience I started to run workshops to teach others how to do it more effectively (how that came about I will describe in a later chapter) and now I've actually had the temerity to write a book about it! I know, you're thinking - 'what a w#nker'!

Well, perhaps it is best to view this publication not as the deluded ramblings of a man who thinks he's it, but more a beginners guide to networking written by a beginner. Yeah, that sounds good; I'd buy that for a tenner.

I'll go into more detail in a little while but all you need to know right now is that, alongside running my own SME (small to medium enterprise) I'm also an actor and this time two years ago I came out of a Christmas show to nothing.

My immediate future could best be described as having an abundance of availability and not much more. I had no money, no hope of making any and no one to talk to about it, no one who might be able to offer me some support or understanding or advice. In short, I was in real trouble.

You see my business, Improve On You – presentation skills and personal impact coaching (www.improveonyou.co.uk) was at a standstill and had been for the previous year if I'm honest.

I had no idea of what to do to breathe life into it and spent each working day sitting in front of my computer screen, limp with inertia, crippled with a dreadful sense of failure and pale-faced at the thought of my dwindling bank account. (Not good when you consider that I coach people to have greater self-confidence!)

Jump to today, right now; 5.20pm on 6 February 2015. I came out of my Christmas show in January to my most successful month for Improve On You so far and I have bookings that take me right the way through to September working with various types of clients from investment companies to bespoke tailors, from local authorities to a high street store and from SMEs to international corporations.

Even as I write this I can't quite believe the steep rise from absolutely sweet FA this time two years ago to the gentle steady increase in the work that is coming in for me and my business.

On top of that, this year I returned from pantomime to a lively social scene populated by like-minded folk, all of whom were happy to hook up and get me back up to speed on all that was happening in the local area.
I didn't arrive back to a wall of despair and isolation but to the warm embrace of a bunch of helpful, enthusiastic mates.

Don't get me wrong, I'm not driving around in a gold-plated Rolls Royce lighting Havana cigars with ten pound notes, far from it - but I'm making a living now when previously there was no living to be made.

Now I've got a circle of new friends and business associates when before I was stuck on my tod and, perhaps most importantly, I have a true sense of excitement about the future when two short years ago I dreaded the thought of what I was going to do with the next ten minutes.

So what's the big difference?

Networking!

Networking with commitment, common sense, good manners, generosity and gratitude.

I want to say at this point that there are a number of other brilliant books alongside this one that are a terrific guide to networking and they are all worth a read.

The classic 'And Death Came Third' by Andy Lapota and Peter Roper; the very recent 'Business Networking for Dummies ' by Steff Thomas, a networker of some 10 years experience and lastly, my personal favourite; Brad Burton's 'Get Off Your Arse'.

All these books are similar in that they cover the business of networking and how to do it right as, indeed, does this lofty tome. But this book is unique! Because this book tells my story of what you as a novice networker are about to experience.

I may only be two steps ahead of you but I can confidently lead the way.

So follow me as I share what I got right and what I got wrong. I want you to learn from my mistakes, glory in my mini triumphs and finally exalt in just how ace I actually am.

I'm kidding of course. I *am* ace but that is beside the point. No, the *point* is...if I can do this you can do this and *you* can be ace too! More than that, you can have a business that is going places and have a true sense of excitement about the future.

Just to explain, this book is split into three distinct parts; the first part Networking and me – Networking and you, deals with how my business was not functioning before I started networking, how I made my decision to start networking in the first place and then a step by step guide through my first ever networking meeting. I want to help you become familiar with what to expect and how to handle all the various challenges you will face when you are in the same situation. This part ends with a crash course in presentation skills to get your 60 second pitch up to scratch.

The second part, Networking Know-how, covers various ways in which you can enhance your ability to network and better succeed in generating income as a result.
In the third part, Networking online - networking in life, I go into the different networking groups that are out there in the hope that you will have a head start in choosing which will be best for you. As well as that I discuss social networking online and how it can be used as an extremely potent tool in the further development of your professional relationships.

And now, as with all good finales, I would like to finish with a song – a song that I sing to myself before I go into every networking meeting I attend. I sing it (yes, out loud) because it makes me laugh, it cheers me up and works as a hugely effective positive affirmation.

I am ace, I am essence,
I am the greatest, I am the best
I am ace, oh yes, I am essence,
So why would you settle for anything less?

OK, that was the end.

This is the beginning........

Chapter 1

It's all about you

(Well, me actually!)

Yes, it's the bit where I talk about me and my career before I set up Improve On You.

Now, as an actor, I have to tell you that I will have to fight every instinct to make this a slow, warm stroll through the softer corners of my life as a luvvie. So, in brief:

I started as a professional at the age of thirteen when I landed the role of The Artful Dodger in The West End production of Oliver back in 1978. I then did a couple of years as a walk-on in Grange Hill alongside Tucker Jenkins and Trisha Yates (who actually fancied me, so there! Trisha, not Tucker!!). Then followed a few years when I 'fell between stools'.

That basically means that as I grew older I became difficult to cast so I went through a fallow period. This happens to every actor throughout his or her career and it was the first of many times that it happened to me.

At sixteen I signed up with an extras agency in an attempt to get my Equity Card (Equity, for those who don't know it is the actors' union and back in those days it was a closed shop and getting your card was a big deal) and for the next two years made mostly invisible, often minuscule but occasionally noticeable appearances in such TV shows as Dr Who (leading Peter Davison to his medieval chambers while wearing a wig that made me look like Barry Manilow), Alas Smith and Jones (with a paper bag over my head), The Gentle Touch, A Fine Romance, Only Fools And Horses and Allo Allo!

During those two years I saved up enough money to put down a month's deposit on a rented flat in London. At the wisened old age of eighteen I left home with twenty quid in my pocket and one suitcase into which I managed to stuff my record player plus a few LPs; oh yeah and a change of undies (probably).

So I was all ready to go. Then followed the main body of my life as an actor. Over the last four decades I've pretty much done a bit of everything - no feature films though. Tons of theatre including West End musicals, Opera, Shakespeare, Brecht and Moliere. I've played two cats, a bear, a fox, a rat, a mole and The Cowardly Lion. Over the years I've shot about 30 commercials and have made the odd TV appearance in shows such as The Bill, Family Affairs, Casualty, Doctors and most recently Hollyoaks.

I love being a performer but, as most will tell you, being an actor is great but being an unemployed actor is bloody horrible. It's a statistic that has been trotted out many times that most actors only work for about a third of any given year.

I pat myself on the back that my overall batting average is well above that, but I've still had to face the challenge of what to do when I wasn't working more times than I would care to admit.

As a young lad, new to London, I did all the things you would expect of an up-and-coming performer waiting for his big break. I worked as a waiter, an usher and a barman. Then there were the more obscure jobs. I was a warehouse man, a painter and decorator, I spent a couple of weeks on a potato riddle and then, on and off for about six years, I was a karaoke presenter (Summer Loving and Unchained Melody have been forever ruined for me as a result but God did I have a laugh!)

The one thing that links all of these jobs is that they were stopgaps. The hours were flexible and when an acting job came up I could leave at the drop of a hat and, if I was lucky, pick it up again when the curtain came down, great for a young, free and single chap who had no commitment to anything other than his acting career.

Then three things happened to me that I had made no sensible contingency for. One was fate, one was the joyous consequence of fate and one was the unavoidable result of both.

I fell in love, I got married and I grew up (sort of).

If all that wasn't enough, my wife Nada and I had a bouncing baby boy and my path to true adulthood was sealed, there was simply no avoiding it - knickers!

Now I had to somehow come up with a job that would fit in between acting work that would pay significantly well and have a future attached. That's how I ended up going into the world of corporate training.

An acting mate of mine had set up a training business and invited me to work alongside him. I worked with him for the next seven years, harmoniously dovetailing training work between my acting jobs. When I was cast as Harry in the West End production of Mamma Mia, I said a fond farewell to being a trainer and was able, for the next three years, enjoy being nothing other than a performer.

Halfway through my time in the West End, I decided that when the job was done I wanted to take the next step and set up a training company on my own. So while still performing, I studied for a diploma in NLP and read vast amounts of source material so that when I left the show I would be ready to go.

The curtain fell on my final performance of Mamma Mia on June 11, 2011 - and that's where the trouble started.

Why am I going on about myself so much?

Well, there is a very good reason. Of course, it has been great fun for me to fall into a reverie about the glories of my past by way of introducing myself to you, but in so doing I have gone through a very useful exercise.

I have retraced the footsteps of my life and taken stock of all my outstanding achievements and now I want you to do the same. I'll explain the value of doing this at the end of the next chapter – which you are going to write! Set aside at least an hour with no interruptions to do this.

In writing chapter two, I want you to go through all the achievements of your life that have made you proud, whether they be in your private or professional life. Go into detail (much greater detail than I went into – I know I'm fascinating but there is a limit). Recall how these achievements made you feel at the time. What is it about them that made them special? Avoid being modest at all costs and avoid being self-effacing in any way. I want this to be a real celebration of everything and I mean everything that you ever got right!

Now go for it.

Chapter 2

It's All About Me! (you actually)

Pen at the ready?

And at the bottom of your chapter you can add another proud achievement. You are a co- author too! (Well only partially and there is no money in it for you so don't come knocking!)

On the more serious point of why I asked you to do this and its relevance to you as a novice networker let me explain:

A lot of people who are at the beginning of their networking journey (I think the majority from what I've seen) have been standing at a crossroads in their life and networking represents the first step in the direction that they have finally chosen to take. There may have been a career change or a redundancy (voluntary or otherwise).

They may have decided to turn their back on the rat race and are taking the plunge in making a pipe dream become a reality by starting up their own business or consultancy, whatever the reason for the change it comes with a certain degree of anxiety and the implied risk of failure. On top of that it may well be that success in this new arena is not just desirable but imperative.

For all these reasons it is really important that we do exactly as we have just done: take stock and remind ourselves that we are amazing and talented individuals able to cope with adversity; and that we have sufficient resilience to cope with the tough times before the good times start to roll (which they will).

However, if we aren't careful all we can hear are the negative voices in our heads telling us that it won't work, that we are not good enough, that there is no point in even trying etc. You know the sort of stuff I'm on about. In this state of pessimism we are rendered impotent by all the negative reinforcement we are serving up to ourselves.

The brain is an amazing thing as I'm sure you know, but it's also a funny old thing too (not a very scientific evaluation but one I think we can all key into). It is so good at so many things but it has a strange default when it comes to allowing ourselves to remember what we are good at and as a result we very quickly forget our past triumphs – we forget who we are and all that we have done.

However, if we actively remind ourselves of all our successes we awaken the positive feel good energy of the things that we have remembered.

Think about it like this. When you go into a room and it has a pleasing aroma - fresh coffee, the scent of flowers, freshly baked bread – as you first enter the smell hits your senses and your awareness level is high.

After a few minutes though, your mind has gone onto other things and your awareness of the aroma has vanished all but completely. In fact the only way of heightening your awareness to its previous level is to leave the room and come back in again. Well that's what happens to our memories regarding past achievements and the feelings associated with them - ones of triumph, satisfaction, pride or a keen awareness of our talents and abilities.

But now you have armed yourself with a weapon to combat that strange cerebral glitch. You have just written an aide memoire that you can return to and awaken your 'can do – will do' muscle.

I bet when you were writing your chapter you started to get all fired up. I bet you had a surge of really positive energy as you recalled what you got right. Well, here's the thing. All that you wrote down actually happened. I want you to own that sense of 'can do' positivity as you embark on your networking odyssey.

Also in going back over all you have done and all you have seen, you will have rediscovered the greatest tool you have in your arsenal for success.

YOU!
YOUR STORY!
YOUR LIFE!

I don't know what your job is but if you are an accountant let me tell you - nobody is just an accountant, or a cupcake maker, a Utility Warehouse rep, a solicitor or small business advisor and certainly nobody became any of these things without being one thing first – a person. So my first piece of crucial advice to you – brave and all-conquering novice networker – is this:

Be a person first -
Be your occupation second

Believe me when I say it is the fabric of your personality that will help you forge lasting relationships of meaning and worth as you network. There will be many accountants, cupcake makers, Utility Warehouse reps and small business advisors but there is – and only ever will be – one you.

So having reminded yourself of your triumphs I guarantee that you will read over your chapter and have a flush of excitement and pride about all that you have written there. Own that feeling and know that all you were capable of achieving in the past you are capable of achieving in the future:

Now, today and tomorrow

Good isn't it?

That's enough about you - back to me again!

Chapter 3

How my start-up stopped in its tracks

or

Bewitched, bothered and utterly bewildered!

So my time in Mamma Mia had finally come to a close and it took me a full four months of waiting around for the next non-existent acting job to appear before I got my backside into gear and began building my Improve On You empire.

First things first. I had a website built. Quite a good one actually, nothing too flash but a good entry-level online shop window. Next I had business cards done, a thousand of 'em. Quite good ones actually, nothing too flash but very good entry-level efforts that were well designed and, I felt, sent out the right message.

Then what? Good question. Then what indeed!

The first few months of setting up had been quite exciting; committing to actually getting things started, sourcing my website guy, sorting out all the content for the site, getting things finalised and finally going live.

That was the 'bewitched' phase and it was very short-lived, making way for the altogether far more full-bodied and protracted, agonising and nerve-shredding 'bothered' phase which would last for the best part of eight long, upsetting, costly, ill-advised, heart wrenching months.

I was the typical 'if you build it they will come' start-up merchant. I had lots of enthusiasm, plenty of optimism but precious little business acumen, no strategy, no goals, no targets and, to be honest, no idea.

When the site went live I was practically tingling with anticipation at the thought of all the work that was going to come pouring in. I mean, how could it not? I had populated each page on my website with well-produced, brilliantly scripted, highly entertaining and very funny videos presented by the extremely Ace Paul Ryan (Yes, *ME!* Paul Ryan!)

In them I talked about how I could enhance the communication/ presentation skills of anybody who had the good sense to hire me. But sure as eggs is eggs, no matter how hard I stared at the phone it steadfastly refused to ring. Knickers!

Actually, more than Knickers: flippin' Ada, holy sh#t, Gordon Bennett and finally, yes; effing hell!
February: Nothing.
March: Nothing.
April: Nothing.
At least my business was performing consistently.

I'm slightly over-egging things, there were about three or four bits of work that I managed to hustle plus a public workshop that I set up myself. (Four people came and only one of them was a paying customer). I think it's fair to say no reason to hang the flags out. Every day I would dread the moment when the school run was done and the house fell silent leaving me at home all on my own to worry. I hated being in my office, in the end referring to it as 'The Temple Of Doom'.

Come May time I had the great idea of blaming my website as being the reason for Improve On You performing so poorly and while attending a business training course (huh!), was convinced by a well-meaning but ultimately dodgy website designer that he could replace, enhance and upgrade my site so that within a couple of weeks I would have more traffic than the M25 within minutes of going live. This guy was ace. I mean really, utterly and fantastically ace, even more ace than me! All my problems would soon be solved and things would finally get moving. Happy days are here again!

So my brand new ace web guru pulled down my old, quite good actually, nothing too flash website and set to work on my all new whistles and bells website which would be up and live within two weeks and all for just £150! I mean, what could possibly go wrong?

I had no website for three sodding months – that's what could possibly go wrong. In fairness, when the site did *finally* go live, it looked great and seemed to perform well. It left breadcrumbs, had a landing page, there was a Twitter feed and a slick looking set of drop down menus.

What I didn't know at the time was that the back end was put together like a Heath Robinson egg timer. And as for traffic, well maybe the odd horse and cart!

Now we go to the 'bewildered' stage – month after dumbstruck month of just not knowing what to do to get things going. A friend helped me put together a business plan, which was very kind, but by this stage, frankly, too late. I had given birth to a baby which, despite all my efforts to feed and nourish, refused to grow and I had come to hate it.

Then something incredible happened. The phone rang. It was my agent. An acting job. Thank God! A taste of freedom, however brief and a more than welcome respite from failing to scare up any work for Improve On You. Ten weeks in Scarborough. I was to play Baron Hard Up in Cinderella and Dr Chasuble in The Importance Of Being Earnest. Halle-bleedin'-luya.

The job came and went and before you could say 'was that it?' that was it.

So on January 5 2013 I was back in The Temple Of Doom not knowing what to do to get things going.

And that's when the trouble ended. Or at least started to end.
Another month of bewilderment was to follow. Then one day in early February a very dear friend of mine, Zoe Hill, sick of listening to me doing my best to make things sound like they were going well, as I swallowed back tears of denial, said to me, "There's this breakfast club thing in Tring that a friend of mine goes to.

"It's all people with their own businesses and they swap their business cards and chat about things and have coffee. My friend said 'it's a really good thing to do'."

I smiled and said, 'that sounds like a great idea. I'll do that'. While all the time thinking: 'Not a bloody hope mate. People! In a room! All together! Being nice! Talking to each other! Well not me mate. What a right load of old cobblers!'

You see, in the intervening months between starting Improve On You and failing to make it work I had lost the one thing I was selling; namely self confidence. In place of being open-minded and excited about the possibility of new experiences I had developed an anxiety which disguised itself as healthy cynicism but was, in simple truth, fear.

All the wind had been taken out of my sails and my ego was as flat as a pancake. I had taken so many body blows to my self-esteem that the service I was selling should have been condemned, as it was, to all intents, not fit for purpose. I had reached rock bottom.

I said goodbye to Zoe and hopped in the car to go home. As I drove back I pondered this idea of the business breakfast Zoe had mentioned. I found myself becoming more and more scathing about the whole notion. People meeting other people, for Christ's sake. What people? I mean who are these people? People with nothing better to do than sit around drinking coffee talking with other like-minded people all being nice to each other for the sake of it. People get on my...

PING! Light bulb moment!

People! That was it. Other people! That was the answer. That was what had been missing all along. How could I have been so blind? I had sat myself in the Temple Of Doom for the best part of 14 months in all but solitary confinement unconsciously locking myself away from the key ingredient that I got most of my motivation from. Other people! Other people were great. Other people were fantastic. I loved other people.

My God, above all the people I knew I was the one person who was a people person personified. I suddenly found myself bursting with excitement at the thought of going along to the meeting Zoe had mentioned. I had all I needed; me, my skill set and 974 business cards. I got home, got online and immediately booked myself in. What could possibly go wrong?

I suddenly changed my mind. Not to put too fine a point on it, I bottled it. That's what could possibly go wrong.

I suddenly had a terrible burst of anxiety at the thought of going into a room full of strangers and talking about myself. I was bound to be crap at it. In my mind's eye all I saw was disaster, humiliation and defeat.

POP! Moment of clarity!
Another but altogether more nourishing thought was that I, above every other novice networker, was supremely qualified to deal with this terrible moment of self- doubt.
I was able to identify it as a simple 'fight or flight' response to the notion of going into a situation where I couldn't tell the outcome.

POW! My epiphany!

I realised that everything I teach as a communications trainer I can use on myself so that I can have mastery over my self-doubt, use body language techniques to create instant and lasting trust before I'd even said a word. And last, but by no means least I could utilise all my presentation skills to ensure I gave a great 60 second pitch that would create a positive first impression and lead to a long-term relationship of mutual benefit with anybody I met.

So that's what I did and that's what I ended up teaching people in my No More Networking Nerves Workshop. And that's what I'm going to teach you as we carry on through this book.

Let's go...

Chapter 4

Why a saber-toothed tiger is stopping you from networking

A number of years ago a survey was carried out on social anxiety. It was discovered that our number one fear was having to speak in public and number two fear was walking into a room full of strangers and that, pretty neatly covers what we are required to do on the networking scene.

We enter a room full of those we don't know and within a few short minutes have to stand up and give a 60 second pitch to the lot of them.

It is these two challenges that stop many people in their tracks before they even get started on the networking merry-go-round. It's perfectly understandable.

Why would you pay good money to go somewhere and feel fearful at best or panic-stricken at worst? Because, moving from the short-term anxieties, if you stick to it, networking really works.

It takes time but eventually you will get fantastic results on many different levels so don't allow your fear to stop you doing something that will provide so much benefit to you and your business.

It's also worth saying that the vast majority of people who fall at the first hurdle when considering going out on the networking circuit will, most likely be saying to themselves, 'I just get sick with nerves at the thought of all those people. I'm such a coward when it comes to getting up and having to speak in front of others'.

Well, here's the thing:
You're not a coward – you're a human being!

A good time perhaps to dwell on life's little ironies.
You can be blind as a bat but still have great insight to the human condition like the ancient Greek poet Homer, you can be deaf as a post but still compose some of the greatest music ever written like Beethoven and you can holiday in France for the last fifteen years and still hate the French like my brother Mark.

But here's one last little irony that is so thought provoking, it might just blow your mind:

A part of every newborn baby is 500 million years old!

And without that part we, as a species, would have failed to evolve from anything more than a blob of slop in the primordial ooze.
It is a part of the brain that has one function; to look out for anything that may be a threat to our lives and prepare our body to respond to that threat in two ways – run like hell or fight like crazy.

This part of your brain has many names: The Reptilian Brain, The Snake Brain and The Brain Stem but is perhaps best known as The Fight Or Flight Complex and, believe it or not, it jumps into life when you are about to go into a networking meeting.

What are the 'fight or flight' responses?
Starting with the low grade responses and moving to the hyper-extreme end of the spectrum:

- Shallow breathing
- Rapid heartbeat
- Butterflies in the tummy
- Nervous sweating
- Dry mouth
- Fuzzy mindedness
- Pins and needles
- Nausea
- Vomiting
- Loss of bladder control
- Loss of bowel control
- Fainting

Now, I'm sure there aren't many people who have ended up passed out and covered in their own vomit, urine and excrement just by walking through the door at a networking meeting, but most of us will recognise the first three or four on that list. We feel anxious, nervous and lightheaded when we are outnumbered by strangers and when it comes to actually having to speak in front of them it is very common to start feeling fearful and 'sick with nerves'.

Well let me reassure you what you are experiencing is not fear 'per se' but a series of 'fight or flight' responses. Now that you can recognise them as such you can contain these responses and make them manageable with a few easily applied techniques.

But it does beg the question – Why? Why would going into a room that is full of people we don't know and having to give a short introduction of ourselves be enough to make our 'fight or flight' response kick in so resolutely?

Well, I don't want to be unkind about it but our 'fight or flight' system can be a bit, well, overenthusiastic these days. Don't get me wrong, it's a brilliant piece of kit and without it I wouldn't be here today, (well, none of us would actually) but in certain situations it is, dare I say it - outdated.

To keep the explanation as brief as possible, your 'fight or flight' system will leap to your defence whenever it senses that your life is in danger. The caveman in us all is constantly on the lookout for the modern day version of the saber-toothed tiger. (Trainers always use a saber-toothed tiger when they discuss 'fight or flight' and I'm no different).

In short, back in the day, your actual saber-toothed tiger would hunt down, kill and eat any passing homo erectus it came upon. Now, if you happened to be the unfortunate homo that the saber-tooth spotted your 'fight or flight' responses would kick in to make sure you could run or fight.

If running or fighting weren't viable options your 'fight or flight' would then go to its extreme responses and ensure that you covered yourself in every disgusting fluid and solid you had at your disposal (pee, puke and poo) and make you pass out (play dead), all in a last ditch hope that when the tiger caught up with you it would take one look at the necrotic foul smelling corpse that was you and say to itself, 'well I'm not eating *that* for a start' and turn and walk away leaving you to fight (or flight) another day.

But we all know going to a networking meeting is not a life or death situation. So here's the good news.....

There is no saber-tooth tiger!

(But figuratively there actually is) – sorry about that!

Our reptilian brain is so finely honed to seek out threat, that just going into a situation where the outcome cannot be predicted is enough for it to leap into action. For example, being alone and outnumbered in a room full of people you don't know and then standing up unarmed in front of them all and giving your elevator pitch!

So here is a brilliant technique that I use to keep my 'fight or flight' response within a manageable range and put me in a state of calm before the networking storm.

Seven Eleven Breathing

Remember the shallow breathing that happens when you get nervous? Here's *why* it happens and what is actually going on *when* it happens.

Your 'fight or flight' gives you a burst of adrenalin which makes the heart beat faster, this in turn means you require more oxygen so you start to shallow breath, pulling as much of the stuff into your blood stream as quickly as possible.

At the same time all this highly oxygenated blood is pulled away from your stomach (giving you butterflies) and moved to your arms and legs so that you can run for your life (legs!) or fight like crazy (arms).

We also lose focus in our thinking processes because when fight or flight kicks in it is imperative that we don't 'think' but 'react' to a threat as quickly as possible – and logical thought takes time so we don't do it in a life threatening situation.

The Seven Eleven breathing exercise is a great way to level off the amount of oxygen in your blood stream and replace lightheaded nervousness with an almost instant sense of 'can do' tranquillity. It also banishes the butterflies and helps to keep your mind focussed.

And the good news is:

IT'S EASY!

- Stand up to your full height
- Exhale to prepare for your next full in breath
- Inhale to the count of seven as you raise both arms up by your side so that by the time you have reached the count of seven your hands are above your head
- Now exhale to the count of eleven – using the whole count to slowly empty your lungs and at the same time lowering your arms back down to your sides.

Do this two or three times and you will notice how a sense of calm has descended. Do this before you go into a networking meeting and your butterflies will go and that fuzzy mindedness will be replaced by a secure sense of consciousness. Frankly, it makes you feel a bit blissed out for a moment but then due to the deep belts of air that you have slowly brought into your system you will feel both energised yet at ease. It is a great way to banish that sense of rising dread before you enter a room full of people you don't know (or for me, just before I have to stand up and give my 60 second pitch).

A couple of things to remember as you try this for the first time:

Breathe in and out from your mouth with your lips pursed as though you are blowing/sucking through a straw. This will help you make the inhalation and exhalation last for the full count of both seven and eleven.

The first few times you use this technique *do* raise your arms. This ensures that you will be taking long deep breaths that will go right down to the bottom of the lungs to calm and nourish you.

With practice you will be able to do this without your arms going up and down and then you will be able to do it in a room full of people without anyone knowing!

I've done an awful lot of public speaking in my life to audiences of all different shapes and sizes – from small groups when giving workshops, to a theatre full of people when asked to make a curtain speech after performances of Mamma Mia (yes, I was in Mamma Mia, did I mention that?) The largest number of people I have ever addressed at one time was 15,000 when I had to introduce the cast at a concert at the O2 but out of all of that the most nerve-wracking bit of public speaking I have had to do has been the 60 second pitch. I don't know why it is such a trauma but please believe me when I say, by using the Seven Eleven breathing technique I have always been able to reduce my sense of anxiety to a manageable level and have never given a bad 60 seconds. Some have been better than others of course, but I have never made a total cock-up of my elevator speech including the first one I ever gave at my first ever networking meeting – Tring Together's BusinessMart.

Chapter 5

How to handle your first networking meeting

Tring Together's BusinessMart is a monthly meeting for local sole traders and SMEs (small to medium enterprises) all aiming to meet up and help each other move forward. For a reasonably confident person I was struck by just how nervous I was feeling as I got out of the car and walked towards the venue for my first ever networking meeting.

Its membership covers all kinds of businesses including solicitors, printers, cake makers, accountants and website designers. I mean, it wasn't like I was going in to meet a couple of heads of state and the Pope but I could feel my fight or flight response kicking in like a mule.

So on my approach to the venue I began Seven Eleven breathing to help regain my composure. After a short time I could feel my anxiety levels reduce and strode in with purpose.

One of the reasons I was nervous was that I, like thousands of others, had not learnt to be comfortable when talking about my own business with any level of confidence.

In England we have a cultural imperative to be rather self-effacing. We do ourselves down and find it crucifyingly uncomfortable to self-promote.

I know lots of people who say they can extol the virtues of somebody else's business till the cows come home, but when talking about their own business get tongue-tied before the cows have even left the flippin' shed. Weird isn't it? And I was to discover that I was exactly the same.

As a new face at an established networking group you will find people very keen to introduce themselves and most of the time it's for no other reason than to put you at your ease.

The problem I had was that the minute anyone started to talk to me, my ability to sound like a person having a normal conversation completely disappeared. I didn't know how I was to start talking about presentation skills and pricing and the benefits of the services I provided without it sounding like I was doing a voiceover for the latest DFS advert.

I persevered and, wracking my brains, managed to describe how great Improve On You was in every possible way to anybody who would listen.

But here's the thing, while I was making a lot of confident noises I wasn't really connecting with the people I was talking to.

And here's why – I wasn't talking *to* them, I was talking *at* them. I thought I was doing the right thing by setting out my stall and making it quite clear what I did, how I did it and who I would like to do it for, but actually I was guilty of boring people into submission with a heady dose of dry-mouthed waffle best described as WordBlur.

I forgive myself this mistake largely because I had no one to advise me on how to approach people in this most unique of social situations.

So, buyer of this book, let *me* advise *you*.....

Don't go to talk – go to listen

So, let's say, for the sake of argument, you are standing nervously at the sidelines of a meeting when out of the blue someone approaches you. They make an opening remark and then ask what you do. To avoid WordBlur try saying something like this:

"I run a *'fill in appropriately'* company and wanted to try networking as a way of getting my message out there. Tell me what *you* do."

Simple as that - a brief description of your line of business then ask the same question that had been asked of you moments before. The person you are talking to will then happily give you a rundown of their product or service while you.....

Listen and ask questions

The great thing about this strategy is that it takes all the pressure off you as a novice networker to provide anything other than a listening ear to those who are much more practiced in the art of promoting and describing their business.

Remember:

The best conversationalist is the one who does all the listening

Listening is a very potent way of striking rapport. When people feel they are being listened to they feel they are being treated with respect. So you achieve two things at once – you gain knowledge of what they do and you create the great first impression of someone who shows real interest in others. Also you will stop yourself from falling into a bottomless pit of WordBlur.

Learn from the person you are listening to

How do they describe their business? Do they talk about business at all? When they describe what they do, do they make it interesting? If so, how so? A few will be boring, most will be interesting and some will be fascinating. Learn from all of them. Avoid doing what you have found tedious or irritating in others and pick up the good habits of those you meet who engaged with you, interested you and maybe even entertained you.

Next big tip:

Copy the good habits of others

Once you've done a few meetings using the 'go to listen' strategy you will be much better placed to start telling others about your business by modelling yourself on other networkers you've met who do it well.

Another really good tip while you are earning your networking spurs is...

Don't just talk about work

No, that is not the longest typo in the history of the written word, I mean it:

Don't just talk about work!

One of the key things to learn about networking is that nobody is there to buy what you are selling. Not a soul. Ask yourself this, when you go to a networking meeting do you make sure you go with your credit card? Do you go with a shopping trolley? Your bag for life? Of course not. It is not a buying environment. And when you come to terms with that fact you will very quickly learn to love it because it takes all the pressure off you to be a sales person. When you take the sales away from the sales person what you are left with is the most important weapon in your arsenal – YOU – the person.

It is often repeated but nonetheless true that we buy the person first. We hire, buy from and trade with people we like. So first and foremost just be you.

Talk about things that interest you, join in with conversations that you find stimulating as you would in any other social setting.

It could be a shared interest in films, theatre, football, current affairs, local issues, or One Direction. There aren't many in a group of people who will have a shared and informed interest in accountancy or project management or pension schemes (or One Direction come to think of it). So, I'll say it again......

DON'T JUST TALK ABOUT WORK!

Networking is all about finding common ground with people and gravitating towards them. So take it easy, take your time and take the pressure off yourself. Understand that if you allow yourself to be yourself you will very soon strike a bond with people you feel comfortable with and before long you will be looking for ways to help each other move forward.

Business will come in time once you've created a network of people you have come to like and who have come to like you. Why? Because we help those people we like. Simple!

So just to recap on how I'm coping in my first network meeting. I used the anxiety reducing Seven Eleven breathing exercise and made a confident entrance. I grabbed a coffee and started to babble at people in a fit of WordBlur - couldn't be helped didn't know any better. All in all though, I'm getting involved and starting to relax, just a little bit.

However, after about twenty minutes of talking to people and feeling more and more comfortable my Reptilian Brain was about to be woken up with a nuclear alarm clock and flood my system with enough adrenalin to keep me in fight or flight mode until I had run a marathon and beaten the crap out of Mike Tyson.

Let me explain why.....

The Tring Together meeting was hosted by the very warm and welcoming Vivianne Child who, after a short address to the assembled masses invited everyone to grab some food and sit down. Then those who wished to have the opportunity to make a short announcement to the group were invited to speak.

Short of volunteers on this occasion, Vivianne asked if there were any non-members who wanted to make an announcement as she had a couple of spare slots. Without thinking my mouth opened and, before I had the chance to shut it, out fell two little words that had an impact on my life from that day to this, 'yes' and 'please'.

I had actually chosen to make an announcement to a room full of strangers without any idea of what I was going to say and I was going to have to say it in about three minutes time! AAAAAGGGHHH!

(Chime of extremely dramatic music)
How about that, a cliff-hanger ending! My God, this book represents value for money.

Chapter 6

How to handle your 60 second pitch

What the hell was I thinking? Had I taken complete leave of my senses? Had I lost all touch with reality or had I taken a couple of gulps out of the cooking sherry before I'd left that morning and felt ready to take on the world?

None of the above.

I had made a cold, hard decision to seize an opportunity that I knew wouldn't present itself for at least another couple of months. Why wait two months and three minutes when in 180 short seconds I could engage with all forty of the Tring Together networkers, introduce myself, tell all of them at the same time what I did and ask for help and advice from anyone who was willing to give it.

Don't get me wrong, I wasn't looking forward to the prospect. Standing up and speaking in front of everyone came with some pretty hefty implied risks; I was going to present myself as an expert public speaker, what if I stumbled over my words, lost my train of thought, came over as diffident rather than confident.

In short, what if it was a nervous cock-up?

'No', I hear you cry.

'This could never be', I hear you insist.

'You are a public speaker with years of experience behind you', I hear you continue.

'You have spoken to innumerable groups of people ranging from pubs full of drunks to black tie charity events. You have presented to numbers as small as one to as large as 15,000. You won't cock it up', I hear you bang on.

'We are the ones who hate public speaking not you. Now just shut up and get on with it you effing drama queen', I hear you forcefully encourage.

'Drama queen I may be', you hear me reply, 'but all that you have just pointed out notwithstanding, I'm only human and I like all of you have a fight or flight system too.'

'So what', I hear you cry, 'you're the expert.'

'That's as may be', I kindly reply, 'I reserve the right to sh#t myself too!'

And that's the whole point of this rather protracted literary conceit.

I may be the expert but I am only human. It is the expertise that I put into practice that sets me apart from those who would freeze like a rabbit in the headlights in a similar situation.

I grant you, whilst it may not have had the same intensity as someone who has never spoken in public before, my fight or flight kicked in like a mule the second I asked if I could make an announcement.

My heart skipped a beat and my thinking became muddled. I realised I had to come up with something quick with regard to what I was going to say but that was the only focussed thought I had before my shallow breathing over oxygenated my blood stream making me feel lightheaded and unfocussed.

Then I noticed a fight or flight response that was only going to make me feel even less able, even less confident: I started to shrink! My shoulders dropped, my chest became sunken and my head went down. This set of R complex physical responses is designed to lower your centre of gravity to help you run and also to make yourself physically smaller so that your predator – let's use the aforementioned saber-toothed tiger – has less chance of actually seeing you in the first place.

The problem with this posture is that within an instant of it being struck it will sap you of your confidence. It will also force you to shallow breathe so that you will not be nourishing the brain with calming, energising oxygen but taking short sharp gulps of air, addling your brain, causing fuzzy thinking and an inability to rationalise clearly.

There is a wonderful and simple solution to this that will make you feel instantly more in control of your breathing, your thought processes and your surroundings. It is so simple and so effective that when you read it you will literally think I am taking the literal p#ss but I promise you I am not.
Ready?

Stand up straight

There you go. Do that and you will suddenly feel the nerves start to dissipate and a sense of calm descend. Honest it is that simple. In his brilliant book, *:59 Seconds* Professor Richard Wiseman tells of how he had a friend who needed some therapy to help her cope with the stress of her hectic professional lifestyle. He agreed to help her and asked how much time she could set aside each day to go through some stress-busting exercises. Her answer? Less than a minute!

For a moment he was flummoxed but then became intrigued by the challenge and so set about designing a set of exercises that would take no longer than a minute to perform that would ease her anxieties and set her along a more balanced and productive path.

Each of the chapters in his book has a scientific explanation (lasting up to twenty pages) of why the exercise would work and at the end he gave the 59 second exercises for the reader to try. His argument being that, yes you could go in to the whys and wherefores of all the research, its findings, it conclusions and outcomes but at the end of the day if you did the exercise without knowing any of it, they would still work. It is a fantastic book that I wholeheartedly suggest you read. He is a brilliant psychologist and creator of quick solutions to lots of problems, but good as he is I have just gone one better. I have created an instant solution. Yes, banish your pre-presentation anxiety by simply standing up straight.

In my No More Networking Nerves Workshop I spend a great deal of time breaking this simple solution down to its component parts and offering all sorts of explanations and reasons as to why it has such an immediate potency in calming our nerves, giving us confidence and helping us to focus but here, now; all you need to know is that if you pull yourself up to your full height all those things will be achieved.

So the moment of truth was nearly upon me. A couple of people had already said their bit and Vivianne gave me the nod to let me know it was my turn next. I took a deep breath, made sure my posture was upright and confident and I put a smile on my face and went for it.

And this is what I said:

'Good morning everybody. My name is Paul Ryan. I run a business called Improve On You. I teach people to speak at their best when they most often speak at their worst. I specialise in presentation training and having worked as an associate trainer took the plunge and set myself up as an independent about a year ago. And I've come here today to ask for your help. I have the skill set and the experience but I have no clue as to how to market myself so I'm really asking if there is anyone here who would be happy to offer me any guidance I'd be most grateful. Thank you.'

What do you reckon? How did I do? Having just read my pitch you might well be thinking, 'Well, the earth didn't move for me', 'Where were the jokes?' 'It was hardly the Gettysburg address.'

What were you expecting? What do you think a 60 second pitch should be? Well, I'll tell you – here is what a sixty second pitch should be:

A quick, succinct summation of what your company does, given in a way that motivates the listener to action.

Nothing more nothing less.

Your pitch doesn't need to be a showstopper or a showcase for your skills as a wit and raconteur. Believe me I have seen many pitches where the person speaking tries to be the new Woody Allen and generally speaking, it doesn't work. The jokes aren't funny enough and their message gets lost in a haze of misguided showboating. So here's another great way of taking the pressure off yourself.

The 60 second A, B, C

Understand right from the outset that your 60 second pitch is not an audition for Britain's Got Talent and, what's more, people don't expect it to be.

As long as what you say is:

A – Audible

B – Brief

C – Committed

Then you will already be standing head and shoulders above the majority of those speaking at your meeting.

There are other ingredients that will greatly enhance these basic prerequisites but if you start with the 60 second A, B, C you will set yourself on the right track to give a solid, professional pitch.

Let me just elaborate briefly.

Audible - speak up and make yourself heard. You won't be putting any undue strain on the voice when you are only speaking for a minute and if people have to strain to hear you they very quickly will stop making the effort.

Brief – avoid running over your time. People get frustrated by this particularly if there are twenty or so speakers.

Committed - make the effort to be emotionally connected to what you say. If you speak enthusiastically people will listen enthusiastically.

What to say

One of the things I see all too often on the networking circuit is people gabbling through oceans of words working under the misapprehension that the more information they can communicate in their minute the better.
Here's what I think. If you say less – and say it clearly – you will always be communicating more. It's not what you say but how you say it and I would always prefer to see somebody calmly setting out their stall rather than breathlessly going through a checklist of everything they sell and all the services they can provide, despite the fact that they are cramming way too much into their allotted time.

In the latter scenario your listener will switch off because your tonal range will be limited by the amount of content you have to get through. You will crowd the ear with rapid speech that lacks variety and have no emotional attachment other than mild panic.

Think about it like this. Hamlet's soliloquy 'To be or not to be' is one of the most thought-provoking and beautiful pieces of writing in the world, but if you try and say it in the space of a minute all its power and beauty are lost and its meaning swallowed up by the speed at which it would be said. Less really is more.

The 5 point structure

Use this simple structure as a starting point for your first foray into the 60 second pitch:

1. Your name
2. The name of your company
3. How long you have been in business
4. A brief description of the services you provide
5. What you are looking for from the meeting

There you go – five things – enough to remember – not too much to forget.

Now go back and read what I said in my pitch to the Tring Together group and you'll see how well this structure works.

This framework will more or less guarantee that you give a small and perfectly formed 60 second pitch. I know it seems a bit rudimentary but it gives you a beginning, middle and end and it will help you to avoid the pressure of having too much to say in too little time.

Also, you are hardly likely to forget the first four points; they being your name, the name of your company, how long you have been in business and what you do. The fifth and last point is where you can allow yourself to be a bit more creative or indeed specific. You can mention a special offer that you have or invite people to come and have a chat with you if they know people who might benefit from your services or, as I did, you can choose to ask for help.

This five point structure is another great way to take the pressure off yourself. I know it might seem obvious to you, but the people listening to you for the first time won't have heard any of it before so keep it lean, clean and verbally un-crowded.

When you plan your pitch using the 60 Second ABC and the simple five point structure you will provide yourself with a firm foundation to introduce yourself to the group in a way that will inform, engage and motivate.

Chapter 7
(or Chapter 6, The Sequel)

Five more great tips on how to handle your 60 second pitch

I run a number of workshops centred on presentation skills. Some of them last an hour, some of them last a morning some of them last a day, so I'm sure you appreciate that there is only so much we can do with two chapters on the subject.

That said, if you take on board all that I put forward in the last chapter and make an effort to use the five tips in this chapter, you will have enough skills and awareness to greatly enhance your ability to give a professional, meaningful and impactful 60 second pitch.

Tip number one:

Hold a cue card

And as a person who is new to doing this, don't be afraid of holding a cue card with your bullet points on. (Bullet points mind you, not everything in your five points written in prose, your card is there to jog your memory if you need it not to read from).

If it helps to have it there for quick reference and puts those nagging thoughts about forgetting what you are going to say at bay, do it! I promise you no one will think any less of you and most who are listening won't even notice.

Please avoid holding a sheet of A4 (folded or unfolded). In my opinion it just looks naff plus if your hands are shaking so will the massive piece of white paper in them. It also gives the impression, rightly or wrongly that you are going to go on for ages (people often do!)

The best thing to use is a plain white postcard with your five bullet points on it. It is small enough to be discreet but large enough for you to see.

Tip number two:

Keep it fresh

Far too many people get up and say the same thing – and I mean exactly the same thing at each meeting they go to. The benefit for them is that they know what they are going to say and so they don't have to cope with the added pressure of new content. However, if people always know what you are going to say they will not listen. This is as true in life as it is in a network meeting.

Think about it, Martin Luther King's 'I have a dream' speech has kept its historical potency because he only said it once (and, incredibly, he made that part of the speech up on the spot). If every time he got up in public and said the same thing, whilst brilliant, it would soon have been viewed as glib.

Instead of a generation held spellbound by the message, people would have slowly turned away quietly mumbling that they had a dream too and that in it the Reverend King was saying something else.

There is one chap I know who always stuck so rigidly to the same script that you could look around the room and see people mouthing along to him as though miming to a record. Not the most charitable response I grant you, but while a few were poking fun there were more who were quickly just ignoring him, using his 60 seconds as an opportunity to check their smart phones or catch up with their neighbour.

On seeing that this poor chap was the butt of some ribbing I quietly took him to one side and gave him some free 'in the moment' coaching, suggesting that he, perhaps, come up with a new angle on the same message.

To his credit he rose to the challenge and from then on continued to bring new content to his pitch (and those smart Alecs who mimed along to him all ended up looking like the total oafs they really were).

So here is a simple way to change your content.

As a beginner I would suggest that – once you have gained sufficient confidence – to add variety, stick to the first three points of the five point structure and change the last two points. Maybe include a recent success story or a customer who had a particular set of challenges that you were able to help with or a business event that you are involved in.

You could even talk about something completely unconnected with your work that has a relevance to the local community or you could ask for a recommendation of services or use the opportunity to make a testimonial to someone in the group. It all helps to keep the listener listening and interested in what you are about to say.

Tip number three:

Look at people when you are talking to them.

I know! It seems obvious doesn't it? But how many times have you watched people get up to speak in public and fail to make eye contact with anyone?

I see it at every networking meeting I go to and the great shame of it is that, no matter how great your product might be or how brilliant your services, if your gaze is fixed steadfastly away from the people you are addressing, your message will not hit your audience with any real meaning.

Did you know that when we speak to people the general rule is that we look away 25% of the time and when we are listening we look at the speaker for 75% of the time? When talking, the reason we look away is to retrieve information from different parts of the brain. When listening we look at the speaker more because we are almost constantly lip reading and taking in the body language to give us a better understanding of the message being sent out.

What does it feel like when somebody is talking to you but not looking at you? Weird right? What does it feel like when someone is talking to you and doesn't stop staring during the whole time that they are speaking? Equally weird and more than a little unsettling, yes?

It's just the same with public speaking.

If you just look at your notes or at the floor or at the ceiling or anywhere else other than at the people in front of you, you will fail to engage with them.

Similarly, if you find a friendly face in the crowd and just concentrate your efforts on them you will freak that person out and alienate the rest of your audience in the process.

It's all about striking the right balance of course and in 60 seconds it would be very strange if you tried to make eye contact with everybody in the room - you would look like a murderous psychopath scanning the crowd for your next victim.

So try this:

As you speak make eye contact with a different person with each different point you make. Five points, five people. Spread them out too. One person at the back of the room, one at the front, one to the right of you, one to the left and finish off picking someone in the middle.

Tip number four:

Do a short vocal warm up

Any actor worth his salt will do a vocal warm up before he goes onto the stage to give his performance. How insulting to an audience to take the liberty of warming up while you are out there! Many do and you can always see them a mile off. They tend to be the ones who lose their voice, make small mistakes and stumble over their words.

Even with an oration as short as 60 seconds think how disconcerting it is when somebody can't be heard or begins by having to clear their throat and then proceeds to pissmronunciate their worms! (A quick nod of thanks to The Two Ronnies for that one).

A typical vocal warm up for an actor might last about ten minutes but for you, my novice networking friend, a few minutes is all you need to wake things up and help your voice to reach out without straining your vocal cords and help you project your voice without sounding like you are shouting.

The King Kong

Take a nice deep breath and start humming on a low continuous note. While you are doing this I want you to gently beat on your chest with both hands (just like that benighted forty foot simian who met his demise at the top of The Empire State Building). You only need to do this for about twenty seconds. This will warm the voice, shift any phlegm or mucus out of the way before you start (cough it up now rather than at the start of your presentation!) it will also help you to achieve a rich, sonorous tone. Doing this simple (if odd) exercise will give your voice more gravitas and help to communicate your authority.

Tongue twisters

When people stand up to give their pitch and say something like 'Good morning everyoddy' instead of the more traditional 'Good morning everybody' they instantly look silly, feel silly and lose credibility.

A brilliant way to avoid stumbling over your words or 'fluffing your lines' is to do a couple of tongue twisters in the car on your way to your networking meeting.

Try these - say them quickly three or four times each while really accentuating the vowel sounds and crunching down on the consonants:

- Wicket cricket critic
- Unique New York, New York unique
- Three free things set three things free

- Equity Deputy
- Red Lorry Yellow Lorry
- One plump lump of sugar two plump lumps of sugar
- Ken Dodd's Dad's Dog's Dead

And if you really think you are up to the challenge:

One smart fellow, he felt smart. Two smart fellows they felt smart. Three smart fellows they felt smart, they all felt smart together.

While you may muck them up and sound a bit silly in the car it's a much better place to feel a bit of a twit than in front of thirty strangers. By doing a few tongue twisters you will have woken up the muscles in your tongue and mouth and, in so doing, lessened your chances of saying 'good morning everyoddy' or something similar. Lood guck thith wiss, sorry, I mean good luck with this!

Tongue and mouth work

Stick your tongue out as far as it will go and point it up to the ceiling then down to the ground. Repeat this three or four times.
Blow a raspberry – a really big fat juicy one. Do this three or four times – more if you find it strangely enjoyable – some do!
Chew an imaginary large toffee.

Roll your tongue around the outside of your teeth quickly five times, then round the other way five times.

Pucker your lips together as though you are about to snog a toad. Now put on a massive fake smile like you are pretending you like snogging toads. Do this three or four times.

When you've done all that, blow air through your mouth and let your lips flap together so that you sound like a horse neighing. Do this three or four times.

There will be many of you who are now convinced that all I want you to do is make you look like a complete prat for no other reason than my own quiet amusement. Not true (not strictly).

In doing these silly but simple exercises you will be warming up the apparatus that you use to shape the sound of the words that fall out of your mouth. Once warmed up you will speak with greater verbal dexterity enabling you to allow the words to come trippingly off the tongue.

Tip number five:
Say it out loud!

In other words, practice! When you have the content of your pitch take it off the page and say it out loud to yourself many times and often. This is something I do when I'm learning lines for a show. I say them fast, slow, loudly and quietly. I say them in a high voice then a low voice. I even say it in silly voices of varying descriptions all in an attempt to get the words deep into my unconscious competent memory.

When the words are at my disposal I can then enjoy saying them instead of simply trying to remember them.

Actors call this 'kicking it around'.

One of the great things about really making an effort to hit different intonations is that you can often surprise yourself with the punch and energy that is created.

Remember you will be just one in a long line of people to get up to speak so anything you can bring to the table to make you stand out is a good thing. Knowing what you are saying and saying it with energy and commitment is a sure-fire way to make people sit up and take notice of you.

Another good thing to do when you are 'kicking it around' is to go off script and see what comes out. I have no doubt you will be amazed by what you come up with. I have done a fair bit of script writing in the past and this kind of extemporising often provided me with some great lines for the characters in my plays.

Take my advice though, if you are going to do this, run a voice recorder so that when you come out with that killer phrase you have it somewhere to refer to. The number of times I have spouted something of genius and forgotten what it was before I could put pen to paper are legion.

So there you are. A potted presentation skills course specifically designed for the sixty second pitch.

Use this stuff, I do, and it really works.

Chapter 8

After the pitch is over

Now where were we? I had just got up at Tring Together and said this:

'Good morning everybody. My name is Paul Ryan. I run a business called Improve On You. I teach people to speak at their best when they most often speak at their worst. I specialise in presentation training and having worked as an associate trainer took the plunge and set myself up as an independent about a year ago. And I've come here today to ask for your help. I have the skill set and the experience but I have no clue as to how to market myself so I'm really asking if there is anyone here who would be happy to offer me any guidance I'd be most grateful. Thank you.'

I have to be honest and say I was being a little cunning in making sure I asked for help. I was banking on our biological disposition as a human race to go to someone's aid when they call for it. And boy did my call for help bear fruit. But more of that later and more on the subject of helping too.

Having given my pitch I sat down, took a gentle sigh of relief and immediately felt the rewards coming in. Yes, immediately. Because here's the good news - once you have given your pitch you are going to feel fabulous.

Believe it or not you will probably want to do the whole thing all over again! Not just because you will have put in place all the tips and techniques from the last two chapters and presented like a true professional but also while you are doing the actual pitch your body will release a little known stress hormone called norepinephrine to help you cope with the situation you have put yourself in.

Norepinephrine is the body's own anti-depressant and, basically, when you are in a stressful situation you will get a small hit of it to lift your spirits to help you cope!

The thing is, once you have given your pitch the hormone is still in your system so, with no stress left to cope with, all you are left feeling is mildly fabulous. In all fairness having stepped up and done your level best, you deserve it – enjoy!

For those of you starting to get a little worried that you are going to fall into an hallucinogenic trance and start running around the place naked on the back of this stuff please accept my assurance that this is not going to happen but there's no doubt about it, you will be buzzing.

Don't freak out! I'm not out to get you hooked. In an attempt to manage your expectations and anxieties on the whole subject of the physiological effects of norepinephrine – if you have ever had any experience on the amateur stage you will be familiar with the feeling of 'coming off on a high.' Well that's all it is, a gentle lift. It's like your body serving up its own gin and tonic and saying 'cheers' to itself after the performance.

Actually, if you want to enhance this little burst of euphoria, certain foods like almonds, apples, nuts and grains provide the building-block materials needed by the brain to manufacture norepinephrine so pack a few of those into your breakfast, give your speech and party, party, party!

More seriously, aside from a hormonal pat on the back there is, of course a greater and far more practical reward. People will have seen you pitch confidently, clearly and well.

Congratulations! You have just created a great first impression on all the people in the room that you have previously never met. A really good pitch will bring people to you so, all things being equal, once the formal part of the meeting is over there will be other networkers keen to come and say hello and find out a bit more about you. This is when you need to remind yourself not to go into selling mode.

Even though people are enquiring about your business it is very unlikely that they want to buy from you there and then, if ever. Really they are enquiring about you.

There may well be an exchange of business cards and an arrangement to meet up for a coffee. All this is good. Networking meetings should act as a first step forum to meet those whom you want to meet up with again outside the strict confines of the network meeting itself.

These follow up 'one-to-one' meetings help to deepen your relationship and scope out how you can help one another move forward. Note that I did not say 'helps you to get someone on their own so you can sell to them.'

I'll say it again, networking is not about selling, it is about creating relationships with like-minded people to mutually assist in the development of your respective businesses. Always keep that in mind whenever you make arrangements to hook up with somebody at a later date.

And all of a sudden it's over

There is an indefinable tipping point that occurs in a networking meeting when instead of saying hello to everybody you meet you suddenly start saying goodbye to them and you may be surprised at how quickly this moment seems to come along. All of a sudden everyone will vanish into the morning in a hail of handshakes and hurried goodbyes. The intensity of these occasions can sometimes leave your head in a bit of a spin and afterwards the silence can come as a something of a shock but nil desperandum – the meeting may well be over but the story has only just begun.

You see, it is what happens afterwards that really holds the value to a committed networker. The intrinsic benefit of the meeting itself is reason enough to get out there and get on with it but for me the added advantage of people contact and all the ongoing benefits that brings actually has greater worth. Suddenly, you're not on your own anymore!

When I first started networking I really enjoyed the flurry of activity that comes directly after a meeting. When you get back home you will have a few emails to send out and, hey presto, you will have received a few too! There will be requests for you to link-in, follow and friend. So much for the solitude of the Temple Of Doom!

Just one word of caution – if you say you will do something – call, email a link, phone somebody to make an enquiry on someone's behalf – whatever it is, make sure you do as you say you are going to do. The minute you are perceived as someone who doesn't keep their word your reputation will be tarnished for at least one person...and people talk. Get a good reputation for keeping your word.

Here's a great networking tip I always make an effort to stick to:

Be a sayer doer!

All the good work you have put into the meeting and the informal one-to-one networking will go for nothing if you are seen to be someone who doesn't follow through. Also, I would suggest that you fulfil your promises as soon after the meeting as possible.

This helps to keep your follow up activity to the same day as your meeting. Not only will you be seen as a quick worker but you can carry on with your day, week, year or, indeed, life without a nagging voice in the back of your head telling you that you let somebody down. Listen, if you went to all the trouble to make such a good impression at the networking meeting why blow it by not keeping your word afterwards.

By the time the meeting in Tring had come to a close I had arranged two informal appointments for a coffee and a chat, one with a social media specialist and the other with an PR consultant; I had a fistfull of business cards and an agreement to discuss one-to-one coaching for a young girl who was about to audition for drama school.

I came away feeling incredibly upbeat and optimistic and decided to join the group. Membership entitled me to monthly email bulletins; entry to two meetings for free and the opportunity to give a presentation to the group should I choose. I go to as many Tring Together meetings as my timetable will allow and after two years I can honestly say not only has it been great fun, most importantly it has helped me to move forward, make contacts in my area and got me involved in other events that happen in the local community.

I know that last bit sounds a little nauseating but it's all networking you know.

When I told best selling author and committed networker Martin Gladdish that I was writing this book he grabbed me by the lapels and demanded that he be allowed to make a contribution about post meeting best practice. Who was I to argue? Here, Martin takes 'Be a sayer doer' to a whole different level.

If you are not following-up, then why bother showing-up?

In business, and with business networking in particular, everyone is looking to stand out from the crowd. Most people at a networking event are rarely the only one doing 'what they do' in the room and even if they are the solitary representative of their profession in attendance it is highly unlikely that they will be the only one of their type that you know.

And yet almost every one of them will tell you about their USP – with the U representing the fact that they 'claim' great service, have lots of experience, always respond to customers quickly, are competitively priced, blah, blah, blah... just like all of the others (no differentiation there then). You see there are very few things in business that are truly unique and that is not the only problem with people's misunderstanding of what a USP actually is.

It is generally believed that USP stands for unique selling point, but that is in fact wrong. It actually stands for unique selling proposition and was a term first coined by a marketing genius called Rosser Reeves back in the 1940s. He realised that 'unique' was an overused idea in marketing for describing 'things' (products and services) and that people are more likely to be influenced by experiences and results. So instead of focusing on the 'thing' that someone was selling, he suggested that the power lay in how its benefits were presented, in other words, in the 'proposition'.

Over time, as with much of the great wisdom of bygone days, people have missed the point (see what I did there?) and misinterpreted the message. It is not about the point – it is about the proposition.

Now what has this got to do with following-up after a networking event?

Most of the people you meet at a networking event, even many of the ones with a polished and professional elevator pitch, will tell you how great their services and customer care is. They will give you their business card and say 'we should meet up some time', or 'give me a call if you need anything', or 'I'll be in touch'. Think for a moment about the last ten people who uttered words to this effect to you. Now, how many of them did you ever hear from again and how regularly have you received a personalised, interesting, interested, relevant and refreshing follow-up email, letter or phone call from someone you met at a networking event? Probably not very often, if ever.

To be clear – I am certainly not talking about the mass email marketing that you will occasionally receive after passing your card to someone else at an event. The stuff which starts with a wacky subject line, waffles on a bit about something the writer saw the other day and ends in a sales pitch...no – I mean that the person you met has taken time to actually do what they said they would do - and get in touch.

Let's say that you've been to a networking meeting this morning with twenty people attending. You listened to each of them, in turn, have their minute or so in the spotlight and you hope that they listened to you too.

Perhaps you had two or three interesting conversations afterwards; either with people that you thought might be able to help you, or people who you were sure could do with your help.

In amongst that there would be the ones who shove their cards into your hand (as though you would care); those who really just want to sell you something and those who simply wanted to chat. You get back to the office with a handful of cards and put them with all of the others, in a folder or in the bin and then get on with your day. Oh, by the way, every single person told you directly or implied (yes all twenty) that they give great customer service etc and most of those 'claimed' that was their USP.

Come the close of the day, or maybe even the next morning, you receive an email. It has a subject line which is relevant to your profession, it mentions what you had talked about in your pitch that morning, it is concise and well written, it has an interesting or valuable message, and it is from one of the people who had told you that they would be in touch. What would you instantly think about that person's proposition – as opposed to all the claims from the others?

The simple action of sending this email puts power and credibility behind the empty words that everyone else merely spoke. It says:

- I listened to you
- I am interested in you

- I do what I say I will do
- I am reliable
- I probably apply the same ethos to my work
- I genuinely want to help
- I am not like everyone else

What you say will never be as compelling as what you do and what you can show that you have done.

So your unique selling proposition should be all about how you deliver the message and when it comes to business networking the most effective thing that you can do is be unique 'after' the event. Before I move on to some practical ideas around exactly how you can do this efficiently, let me leave you with this last thought. Because it is this which will turn the idea of being 'different' into being (very possibly) unique.

Making you the most uniquely reliable 'blank' in your marketplace.

At the start of this piece, I mentioned that the people you meet at networking events will almost invariably be in touch with or, at the very least, aware of others that do what you do.

We then looked at the idea of you standing out from all of the others at an event by being the only one who bothers to follow-up in a friendly, personal, relevant manner.

Well, put those two truths together and you are starting to create a one-way road to a really strong (possibly unique) selling proposition or story.

Not only will you be remembered, you will be remembered as the only (add your area of expertise here) that they know who ever bothered to get back in touch after your first meeting. How powerful would that be? What credibility would that add to your proposition?

If you do not believe me, or you still doubt the truth of this... simply count how many people actually 'get back in touch' as a result of the next networking meeting that you waste time, effort and money going along to!

But I'm busy - how do I make time to individually follow up all of the people I meet?

This response drives me mad to be honest! If you consider all of the time that you spend out of the office engaging with people and talking about your business at networking meetings, social gatherings and other business events, why on earth wouldn't you spend a fraction of the time following up the two or three people you met there who represent an opportunity.

That's right, just two or three people, not all twenty that were there, because not all of them will be right for you (or you for them). This way you save on business card reprint costs and you save ruining your reputation because you only ever make promises that you are certain to keep.

Here is what I do:

- Have a target: at every networking meeting I go to, I simply aim to identify and talk to two or three people who I think I can help or I think might be able to help me. The fact that I am very clear about my target market helps here and I suggest that you think very carefully about yours too.
- Avoid the business card bonanza: I very rarely give my business card to anyone that has not actually asked for it and I only ever take the business card off someone who I feel fits the description above (at a networking meeting – there are other times when card collecting is useful).
- A kept promise is the only one worth making: I never ever (ever) promise to follow up if I don't think the person I am talking to is someone that I can see an opportunity to help or engage with further. I will be polite and speak to them, but (especially if I have spent money and committed time to being there) I am very conscious that I am working and my business is paying for it. So I am always looking for genuine opportunities.
- Take note and take notes: as I leave the meeting, with two or three opportunities to do business in my pocket I make a note (sometimes I do this straight after or even during the conversation) of the most important or relevant things we spoke about: personal interests, business goals, problems, solutions, commonality, future opportunities, needs, areas of expertise or similar...

- When I get back to the office: Later that day, or the next morning I go to my file of networking follow-up template emails and choose the most relevant one. I adapt it to fit the conversation and then press 'send'.
- Follow up the follow-up: Have a plan and a schedule. The only way to find out if there is any future or ongoing value in a relationship which started with a coffee and a biscuit in a hotel conference suite is by keeping in touch and seeing where it goes. So make sure you maximise every opportunity. This could mean connecting on LinkedIn, a phone call, a meeting, a free gift, an invitation to an event or whatever you feel is a relevant level of engagement. But please be different and do something.

A final note about templates

When I talk about templates, I don't simply mean a bog standard 'fill in the name' sales email. I mean a structured email, which is a standard format, but which has a number of key ingredients that will make it very relevant and personalised to the receiver. These key features might include:

- Their first name
- The event and date
- Something you talked about or that happened at the event
- A piece of information or advice that will really help them
- A question that you think they might be able to help you with
- A request for more information about their business

- Suggestions as to why it would be beneficial to them for you to meet up
- Putting forward a few options of when and where to meet

As I mentioned before, I have about four basic templates that I work from, depending on the level of the conversation that we had; whether the opportunity was for my business, for theirs or both; and what we decided would be a good way to take the conversation forward.

I hope that has helped you to see why networking without following-up is, at best a hit-and-miss exercise, or at worst a complete waste of everyone's time. But done intelligently, wisely and regularly can turn your presence at any networking event into a powerful USP, which will grow your reputation and win you more business.

Thanks Martin. A brilliant set of tips from a man who really knows how to cultivate long-standing business relationships through his post meeting activity.

To round off this first part of the book I want to give you one last tip.

Keep going

To get the best out of networking and to deepen and strengthen your relationships with other networkers you must go regularly and often. Turning up once in a while or only every so often will yield nothing for you and you'll never really get into the swing of it either. Networking is like anything else, it takes practice.

And remember..

If you work hard at networking, networking will work hard for you

Part Two

Networking Know-how

Four brilliant ways to strengthen your ability
to network effectively

Chapter 9

How to grow a pair!

I know I've spent a lot of time discussing the stress and anxiety often associated with networking but it is worth remembering that networking takes guts...

GUTS to turn up in the first place
COURAGE to actively push yourself into the fray
TRUE GRIT to introduce yourself to a whole host of people you don't know
and...
NERVES OF FLIPPING STEEL to get up and actually speak in front of them.

So here's one piece of advice that will make the whole process of networking more rewarding and a great deal more exciting should you decide to act on it. When you go to a networking meeting -

Take your balls with you – both of them!
(Yes – you too ladies)

It's weird but if you make the conscious decision to be brave you will feel brave and thus actually be brave. The Fish Philosophy's main tenet is to 'Choose Your Attitude' and the potency of this is all to do with the power of the conscious mind over the suggestive nature of the subconscious mind.

At its most basic the subconscious mind will believe whatever we choose to consciously tell it.

So if, for example, you say to yourself 'I hate the idea of going to networking meetings' you will and what's more you will continue to hate the thought of going to networking meetings. Your subconscious will take the information you have given it and take it as read that what you are telling it is the truth. It very quickly becomes a self-fulfilling prophecy.

Do any of these phrases sound familiar?

I never know what to say to people. (You're right – you won't know what to say people).

I find it really difficult talking about my own business. (Right again – you will find it difficult).

The whole thing just makes me nervous. (Bingo! Nervous you will be).

I just clam up. (You will).

I just don't see the point in networking. (You won't).

These kinds of self-limiting statements are extremely debilitating and must be silenced. They create a negative reality in your subconscious that becomes your external reality and on top of that they keep you nicely cosied into the warm loving arms of the stress-free paradise more commonly known as your comfort zone.

The comfort zone and all that is wrong with it

Your comfort zone is the place in your head where you feel relaxed, at ease and secure. In your comfort zone everything you do is something you have done before. A place where you need not take any chances and make no effort to learn anything new. It is a place best characterised as contented inertia.

Your comfort zone - where all is familiar, where every situation is risk free and where discoveries fail to exist, a haven where you don't need to question what you're doing, what you've done or what you are going to do. Sounds good doesn't it? But be careful. Stay there and you will be hermetically sealed in a world with no surprises; secure in the knowledge that you were right all along! Well done you!

Ask yourself, is that where you really want to be for the rest of your natural born life? No, of course it isn't.

It is fascinating to me that the most common way we use the term 'comfort zone' is when we put 'It's a bit outside my...' before it, as though being outside our comfort zone is to be viewed as a somehow burdensome or a woeful inconvenience – a condition to be treated with sympathy rather than the admiration it so richly deserves.

Be Warned!

Choosing never to venture out of your comfort zone will ensure that you remain static and become stagnant.

Be honest, have you ever used 'It's a bit outside my comfort zone' as the most convenient reason for just not bothering or for not addressing what you find a little frightening? The truth is that we've all done it, including me, but as a novice networker going outside of your comfort zone it is a fundamental requirement if you are going to make an effective impression on the networking circuit.

I've already said in my first year in business with Improve On You I was failing. Any mistakes I made I steadfastly refused to learn from. I kept doing the same thing and kept getting the same result – a big fat zero! Why? Because I stubbornly refused to push myself out of my comfort zone. You see, whilst the Temple Of Doom was indeed a place of solitude and misery it was also a cocoon where I didn't take any risks and as a result I was imploding. You see comfort can very quickly turn to panic if you don't go into stretch and if you don't know what any of the last sentence means, have a look at this:

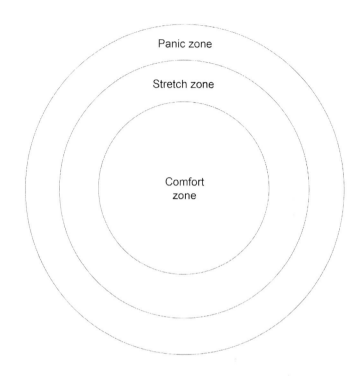

What lies outside your comfort zone?

Philosopher and spiritual leader Neale Donald Walsch wrote:

'Life begins at the end of your comfort zone'

How right he is.

So why don't we like going outside our comfort zone? Because when we do so we raise our anxiety levels which brings on a stress response. I know we don't like feeling anxious and uncertain but it's worth it in both the short term and the long run. Almost immediately you will feel an enhanced level of concentration, focus and stimulation.

With a commitment to having new experiences comes excitement and a real sense of being in the now – present – in the moment. Doing something different, feeling something new is incredibly invigorating and once you get used to it you start to love it. So come with me into the exotic and stimulating world of the stretch zone.

The stretch zone and all that is right with it

Also known as the optimal performance zone – the stretch zone is the place where your performance will be enhanced and where your skills will be optimized and extended. Sounds good doesn't it?

In a way you already have a taste of being in your stretch zone by opting to network. With that decision comes all those fight or flight responses we talked about earlier but now you are armed with a whole host of tools and techniques to combat those feelings.

One of the greatest benefits of the stretch zone is that it really is a place of incredible learning and by going out and using the techniques you have learnt from this book you will gain new experiences and go on to learn from them too. With this broadening of your knowledge base will come a greater confidence, a strengthening of your self-esteem and richer array of colours on your palette of life experience.

In the past two years I have done things I have never done before, become friends with people whom I never thought I would have anything in common, swallowed hard when taking risks and smiled broadly when the risks paid off. I have also run in three sprint triathlons, three half marathons and look, I'm writing a book, all because I took one step from my comfort zone into my stretch zone. I feel more accomplished, more stimulated more alive and braver than ever before.

What Lies Outside The Stretch Zone?
The Panic Zone

Now as a networker you will never be in an environment where panic will be induced (unless you suffer from Anthropophobia – the irrational fear of people or society) so you might be thinking this, the darkest of all the zones, is something you needn't worry about.

However, check out this scenario:

You are a caveman. It's a cold day on the savannah and you are nice and cosy in your cave. In the distance you can see the outline of that flippin' saber-toothed tiger we mentioned earlier. It's still a way off so instead of going into your stretch zone and leaving the warmth of your cave to find a place of safety you don't do anything. The next time you look up the tiger is almost upon you. What are you going to do? Panic of course. And then get eaten.

Or how about this one:

You are the owner of your own small business concern. You know that your business is struggling and would benefit from you going out on the networking circuit but instead of going into your stretch zone and giving it a go you stay in your comfort zone and don't bother. Your business venture fails. Then what are you going to do? Panic of course. And then get your house repossessed.

The best way of avoiding panic and the pain of crisis is to grow a pair and go into stretch, make new discoveries, meet new people; open up new avenues of opportunity and new income streams.

Yes, you will occasionally suffer the discomfort of making mistakes and getting it wrong. But guess what, with every mistake you make you will have learnt something.

So how do you grow a pair?

Henry Ford famously said: "Whether you think you can or you think you can't – you're right."

So think you can!

Here's how:

Positive affirmations

First let me explain what a positive affirmation actually is. An affirmation is an assertion that something exists or is true. A positive affirmation is, quite simply, one that is framed in the positive.

Using positive affirmations is an extremely effective way of retraining the brain to think more positively more of the time. If you have a negative thought replace it with a positive affirmation. This will immediately make you feel less stressed and give you a positive mindset which will empower you rather than cause you to doubt your own abilities.

One rule: they must always be set in the present and must be within the bounds of reality ('I'm going to win the lottery' is a wish not an affirmation!)

I'm a big believer in positive affirmations because, hand on heart, I can honestly say that since using them I have never given a bad audition, always given a respectable 60 second pitch and consistently raised myself to the challenge of every business meeting where the stakes were high.

It is worth saying that I still hear the negative voices in the back of my head before an audition or when I am about to speak, or as I sit and wait in the reception for my prospective client. But now I know these voices are merely the fight or flight system looking for areas of danger. That said, they can be very debilitating if I keep listening to them. However, now I know what to do to silence them. I always use positive affirmations to break the negative narrative and induce calm and confidence.

So let's reframe the self-limiting, negative affirmations we used at the beginning of this chapter to self-empowering positive affirmations.

'I never know what to say to people'.

Reframe to:

'I speak confidently and well at networking meetings'. (Now you will).

'I find it really difficult talking about my own business'.

Reframe to:

'I speak with an infectious enthusiasm whenever I am asked about my business'. (Now you do).

'The whole thing just makes me nervous.'

Reframe to:

'My confidence is growing with each networking meeting I attend'. (Now it is).

'I just clam up'.

Reframe to:

'I am open, interested and interesting'. (Now you are).

'I just don't see the point in networking'.

Reframe to:

'Networking offers great opportunities for the growth of my business'. (Now it does).

These are only examples for you to see how easy it is to turn a negative thought into a positive one. My advice is to listen out for your negative thoughts and immediately reframe them into your own self-empowering positive affirmations.

There are a number of simple ways to use your positive affirmation. You can write it down a bit like when you were given a hundred lines at school. You can just make the conscious decision to think it over and over again – repetition is very important and I would also suggest gently nodding your head while you do this. You can say it out loud like a mantra. You can write it down on a post it and stick it up where you can see it. A really great way of hearing your positive affirmation is to imagine somebody you admire whispering it in your ear.

Every time I am sitting waiting to go into an audition I use the positive affirmation, 'I am sharp, polished and professional' before an interview, 'I am calm, confident and focussed' and they work a treat.

Remember, your unconscious mind will make a reality of what you tell it so help yourself out by telling it positive things rather than negative things. By using positive affirmations you can become braver, reduce your stress levels, worry less and most importantly, as a networker, inhabit your stretch zone and feel all the benefits of doing so: go to that meeting feeling energised, start up conversations with confidence, speak fluently and in an engaging way, arrange one to one meetings and feel the excitement of taking small risks. Do all of this and see your business grow.

Caution!

There is one last observation I want to make about the comfort zone. It has a gravitational pull! I know this from personal experience.

Having moved into my stretch zone and gone to my first ever networking meeting with the Tring Together networking group I very quickly got used to what it was, what happened when I got there and what to expect when the meeting was over. The problem was that within a couple of meetings I was back in my comfort zone. I loved going along, enjoyed meeting the people, gained the benefit of regular attendance but failed to venture out further.

Tring Together was the only networking group I was attending. Wrong! If you are going to commit to networking you must attend as many meetings as you sensibly can.

Remember...

With limited networking come limited results

But then I got lucky. I got myself a wingman!

Chapter 10

My Wingman

As you make your way around your networking circle there is every chance that you will meet somebody who you really click with. When you find this person my advice is pool your resources and reap the rewards of going into networking meetings with an ally, a compadre, a wingman - or indeed a wingwoman!

It is worth saying that the next stage in my networking evolution was not something of my own creation. It was not something that I had planned, conceived or even contemplated. But it was something that came about as a direct result of my first fledgling networking efforts.

I went along to the Tring Together networking group and bumped into the bloke who had designed and printed my first run of business cards, Mark Collingwood.

By this time he was working as a sales manager for a company that created high-end bespoke websites. I didn't know him that well but it was a pleasant surprise to see him. When he got my cards sorted for me he seemed like a really nice guy. In the networking scenario he was one of these chaps who people immediately warmed to. He had a great smile, a playful sense of humour, he wasn't pushy and he knew his stuff.

So, we got chatting and it turned out that, like me, he had only been on the networking scene for a couple of months but unlike me he had really gone the whole hog with regard to how many meetings he was attending. While I had been to three meetings (all at Tring Together) he had been to about 15 in the same space of time. I commented on how I was amazed by his commitment. His response was to ask me a question that was to take my networking activity from first gear to full throttle. 'What are you doing tomorrow? Do you fancy going along to the Biscotti meeting at Amersham?' (Biscotti is a non-subscription group with branches all over the country – but more about them in part three).

I accepted his invitation and the next day we embarked on a two-a-week networking spree that was to last for about eight months.

It was brilliant and we are both feeling the benefits of each other's moral support, areas of expertise and extended network of people right up to this very day. So here's the big tip:

Get yourself a Mark Collingwood
(Not actually him but your own version of him)

One practical advantage of buddying up with someone is fairly straightforward; you can lift share and split the petrol.
This in itself is of serious financial benefit. Hawking yourself around a 35 mile radius two or three times a week comes with a fairly high fuel bill. If you can split that 50-50 with someone, you are taking the sting out of that expense right away.

Beyond that there is a far greater long-term emotional benefit this simple arrangement will facilitate. It will come into play at the beginning of every networking day – and its value is incalculable.

We all know what it is like in a car with a mate. You talk, you listen, you give advice, you take advice, share opinions and come up with schemes, strategies and develop a shared approach to the job in hand.

If you got out of the wrong side of the bed that morning you have someone right there who will help to lift you out of your mood and put you in a better mental space.

We all have bouts of pessimism but if you are lucky enough to get yourself a wingman I guarantee they will take it as their duty to cheer you up and set you straight. When travelling with a wingman you both get a free therapy session before you get to your networking meeting.

Encouragement is a hugely potent thing and as you travel to your meeting you will be offering encouragement to each other in all sorts of ways, so that by the time you get out of the car you are all set to go. All negativity and self-doubt will be left outside so that when you go into your meeting you will be brimming with quiet self-confidence.

Another immediate advantage is that going into a meeting with your wingman by your side is never as daunting as when you have to go in alone. If all else fails you at least have each other to talk to so you will never be stuck on your own in a corner, not venturing to introduce yourself to anyone and looking like a networking wallflower.

As you stand together in conversation you can keep your eye out for those who may look uncomfortable or stranded and invite them to join you. In welcoming someone in you will be creating a great first impression and together you and your wingman can find out all there is to know about that person while taking the opportunity to reference your own businesses without being pushy.

It's also worth saying that you can keep each other's backs as well. Not all those who go to networking meetings will be the type of person you will want to spend time getting to know. If you meet someone who you have found to be pushy, predatory or unprofessional you can warn each other off them.

See more – hear more

The maths is quite straightforward here. If there are 20 people at the meeting and you both get to speak to five each, you have doubled your room coverage jointly, making connections with 50% of the attendees as opposed to a more modest 25%. When there are two of you working as one you can get a better idea of where synergies may be apparent that could benefit you or your wingman so, in effect, you are in two places at once.

You may begin a conversation with somebody and know instantly that this person has more in common with your wingman. Very quickly you can make an introduction and pave the way for a conversation that may one day lead to some business being created.

Then there is the other immediate benefit of being able to introduce your wingman to people at a networking meeting that you have met previously. Remember the whole idea is to build up a network of people who you can call on, recommend and rely on when you need to.

It is not about gathering as many acquaintances as you can and keeping them in isolation from each other. There is no value in this. Working with your wingman you can more speedily enhance the strength and size of your network and thus benefit from it more readily.

In business we have all heard the expression:

'It's not what you know, it's *who* you know'

Well, with networking there is an even greater truth:

'It's not who you know, it's who *they* know'

Remember you are never selling to people when you go networking, but if you consider that each of those people you meet will comfortably maintain 150 stable relationships in their lives you can see the extended potential of each encounter you make when you go into the network environment.

Again, the maths here is simple. If you and your wingman come away from a meeting having jointly made connections with ten people you have paved the way to being recommended to 1,500 individuals who may one day have a need for your product or service. By strengthening your relationship with the right person you meet on the circuit you are greatly enhancing your chances of being recommended to the 150 people they know while creating a new friend at the same time.

Remember:

Enhance your relationships
To enhance your sales

Give and take

One of the advantages Mark and I found in each other was free exchange of services. We helped each other out in any way we could with the skills we had.

Interestingly, while Mark was a great one to one networker, he failed to shine when he was giving his 60 second pitch. I was able to offer him a free seat at a number of presentation skills courses whilst giving him private tuition alongside his classroom learning, to really enhance his ability to both speak in public and strike lasting rapport when meeting people for the first time.

In return, Mark went on to design any leaflets I might need from that day to this and when I had run out of my first set of business cards he redesigned and arranged the printing – all for free.

The immediate saving for me was significant and the long lasting value of the coaching I gave him has had a hugely positive impact on his ability to create leads through networking. A win-win situation for both of us.

But this is the gift that keeps on giving.

The quid pro quo, the contra deal or good old-fashioned 'I'll scratch your back, you scratch mine' are all perfect examples of how one hand washes the other.

Yes, you get the advantage of getting stuff for free from your wingman, but at the same time your wingman gets the benefit of you gaining a deeper understanding of what they do, how well they do it, their approach to their work and vice versa.

So whenever the opportunity should arise where Mark and I could recommend each other to people we met on the circuit, we were doing it from the point of view of being informed customers (except we didn't have to pay).

Recommending each other

Once you have been on the circuit for a while and proven yourself to be trustworthy and honest you will have built up a large number of networking acquaintances who will value your opinion.

Remember, people buy people and when they have bought into you they will buy into whoever you recommend. When you reach this stage what better form of advertising for your wingman than word of mouth?

If and when you see an opportunity to recommend your wingman to someone who has a need for their services, your recommendation will have a far greater authority by sheer virtue of the fact that the endorsement has come from you.

If this sounds at all manipulative or underhand think again. I would not recommend anybody unless I had complete faith in them. Why would I want to?

If someone I recommended fell short of what was required it would only reflect badly on me. So assuming that both you and your wingman are honest players there is absolutely nothing wrong in pushing somebody forward in whom you have faith. In fact, whenever I recommended Mark I felt I was enhancing my own status because I knew the service his company provided was premium.

I know of at least three clients that Mark secured on the basis of my recommendation and from Mark's point of view he has brought a continuous stream of clients to my various workshops, he has also brokered meetings with companies who have needed presentation to camera coaching. He introduced me to those of his clients who have required a voice over artist to narrate their online videos and has put me forward as the 'go to' guy for anybody in need of communication skills enhancement.

He's happy, I'm happy and all our respective clients are happy. What's underhand about any of that?

You can both do the washing up together

When the Networking meeting is over and you are back in the car you can go through the process of 'the wash up', whereby you compare notes and share any information that you think might be useful for your wingman to know.

You can both take stock of the meeting - what you learned, how people came across and if you think there is point or profit in pursuing any relationship.

Many times there will be the situation where you have both had individual conversations with the same person. After the meeting you can then share a frank exchange of views on what you felt about that person.

It's amazing that when you spend time with someone with whom you share a genuine rapport you tend to be drawn to the same type of people. There will, however, be the odd occasion where you both feel differently about someone you have met at a meeting.

But here it is worth remembering that words are the mother of thought and if you feel negatively towards someone but your wingman holds an opposing view a healthy discussion can help you both solidify your thoughts.

Neither of you may change your mind, but you will have had a chance to bounce your ideas around and create a more balanced view. Your discussion might confirm what you felt or it might make you change your mind completely but instead of going home on your tod and feeling ambivalent toward someone you will at least have talked it through with a person whose opinion you value.

What does my wingman think?

As I couldn't have written this chapter without the experiences I shared with my wingman, I decided to ask Mark what he thought the benefits were of our time on the networking circuit together.

Unsurprisingly, he broadly covered all the stuff I have written about so far, but then through our discussion he pulled out one element of having a networking partner that I think stands as the primary advantage of having a wingman.

Accountability

Mark highlighted how hard it can be to stay continually motivated when you are running on your own steam. Solitude can sap your energy. When you sit with your own thoughts, the law of entropy can turn the brightest optimism to the most bitter pessimism and when you are not accountable to anybody its too easy to 'put things onto the back burner', 'let things slide' or talk yourself out of doing the things that you know in your heart of hearts should be done and when we turn our back on ourselves our self-esteem can hit rock bottom rapidly.

By having a wingman you can talk your ideas through with somebody whose opinion you respect. It is a highly valuable and effective way of bringing your thoughts into reality and letting somebody you trust analyse them. A good wingman will offer you praise when an idea is good and give honest, constructive criticism if an idea is bad.

Once you have crystallised your objectives you help each other set goals, keep on top of each other to make sure you keep moving towards your goal and when that goal is reached you can offer each other sincere congratulations, a well-earned slap on the back and maybe even the odd pint! You can glory in each other's victories, however small they may be. Offering each other big celebrations of small wins will eventually lead to massive celebrations of big wins.

Mark rounded off by saying that in his view, the best thing a wingman can offer you is accountability – yes, to them – but ultimately to yourself.

I would like to end this chapter by offering a distillation of all that my time on the circuit with Mark has meant both as a networker and eventual close friend - and it is this:

The Wingman Philosophy

Your wingman is a confidante, confessor, therapist, coach and mentor. He will provide support, encouragement and honesty in equal measure. He has a steady hand, a listening ear and a shoulder to cry on. He will advise and deliberate, he will console and commiserate and he will excite, enthuse and celebrate. It is a two-way relationship on a one-way street to mutual success.

As a brilliant postscript – at the start of our wingman adventure Mark had just begun as a sales manager for a web design company. Through his networking he built up a huge roster of satisfied clients and helped his business boom.

As a result he was headhunted and is now a partner in the online marketing company Digitally Engaged. You can never tell how it will serve up the goods but I'll say it again…

Networking works!

Chapter 11

Business cards and what to do with them

I'm guessing that you have a business card of your own. Go and get it and have it in front of you as you read through this next chapter and decide if what you're holding is really working in your favour.

If you haven't got a business card yet you can use this as a guide to help you come up with a card that is a true reflection of you and what you do - reflection being the operative word here because any business card good, bad or indifferent sends out a message to the recipient of how you approach your business. So if it is well thought out, with a professional design, clear messaging and good to the touch you will already be sending out a great message that will reflect positively on you.

On the other hand if it's cheap, poorly produced, stuffed with too much content and printed on the flimsiest of card you will be sending out a very different message and your business card will act as a poor reflection on how you approach your work.

There are exceptions but a good rule of thumb regarding your business card is:

Buy cheap, look cheap

So don't do it!

And never, never, never use business cards that you can get for free. Yes, they can actually look quite good, the print is of acceptable quality but on the back they always have an advert for the company that printed them i.e.

'Business Cards are FREE at Pistaprint'

Your business card is there to advertise YOU not THEM. Plus you will just look like a total cheapskate amateur. Is that how you want to be perceived? Of course not!

So don't do it!

Invest in yourself so others will be encouraged to invest in you too. It is very important that you have confidence in your business card so that each time you hand one out you feel a sense of pride.

In a very real sense when you give someone a business card you are saying 'this is me'. Decide what you want that person to think of you because every time they see your card they will be thinking the same thing - so do all you can to make sure they think positively.

Here's a controversial statement ladies and gentlemen:

Size does matter!

The most commonly sized business card is your standard three and-a-half by two inches.

You can then get postcard sized, mini cards, cards that fold out and more intricately designed cards that do amazing things. I saw one recently that pulled out to add oars to a rowing boat that actually went up and down as though they were moving through the water!

But here's the thing; little ones get lost, fold out cards are bulky and frankly a bit irritating and big ones just get in the way of things. The rowing boat was fantastic so I'm not a total misery guts on the subject – of course there is room for creativity and playfulness where appropriate, but as a regular networker I prefer the standard size. It's less fussy, more direct and more easily stored.

However, the three and-a-half by two does come with its own challenges. It's not a lot of room to play with, which is why it is so important that you give careful consideration to what you put on it. A really good starting point is to decide what you want the recipient to get out of it and go from there.

The obvious things are all your relevant contact details:

Your name, company name, phone number, website address, Twitter handle/YouTube channel, your strap line.

Ideally, you will only have four or five lines of text properly laid out and legible. I see so many cards that are overstuffed with information printed in a font size that is so tiny that I can't read it – avoid this. It tries the patience of a saint when you have to re-enter somebody's email address a number of times because you can't see the words – it's annoying!

Branding

It is vitally important that you have the same branding on your card as you have on your website, your letter headings and any promotional gifts that you may have (pens, balloons etc.) So the same logo, colour scheme, photography and type settings please. If these don't match, your brand lacks uniformity which will jar when somebody goes to your website from your business card. It also sends out a message that you are doing things piecemeal, one thing at a time with no overview of the message that you want to send out. A lack of co-ordination in this respect will, again, make you look like an enthusiastic amateur at best or, at worst, just plain sloppy.

Should you have an address on there?

Opinion on this is divided. On my first 'quite good ones actually, nothing too flash' business card I was advised to include my address. This wasn't an office address or a PO box but my home address. I was a sole trader so why not? It seemed to make good sense.

One night I was travelling back from London and bumped into an acquaintance of mine on the train. We hadn't seen each other for a while and he asked if I had any acting work. The answer was a sorry 'no' but I enthusiastically began to tell him all about how I was setting up Improve On You.

It turns out that he was a business advisor and he very quickly went into work mode. 'Let's see your card then', he asked rather a little too abruptly for my liking. I warily handed one over and immediately crumpled at his withering stare.

'Right, OK, well this looks sh#t. Never have your home address on there. It makes you look like a one-man band, a small timer. No one will take you seriously looking at that'. I took a deep swallow, thanked him for his feedback and then fended off his offers to provide business coaching at a 'reasonable but respectable monthly retainer'.

Now, obviously, there was a certain amount of self-interest in the frankness of his appraisal but it struck me that he might have had a point.

The next day I sought the advice of someone who I had met on the networking circuit (see, I had someone to turn to for advice unlike my previous non-networking situation - networking working on more than one level!)

He point blank disagreed with the guy I'd bumped into on the train, which came as a great relief to me (I had 1,000 of the flipping things printed, remember). His reasoning was simple. 'It's another point of contact. Another way of getting in touch with you should people want to. Keep it on there'.

So really, you have to decide what works best for you. It is worth saying though that when I had my card redesigned I took off my home address.

Should you have your photo on there?

Guess what? Opinion on this is divided. Some will say that a business card should be about the business not the person, but as a sole trader or leader of an SME you are the business and people are primarily buying into you.

As a person on the business networking circuit I would suggest that a good headshot is of real benefit when you consider that after a meeting your business card will be one of a number that a person might walk away with. If that person gets home and puts your card on a pile of other cards to be logged at a later date there is every chance that when they get round to doing it they may have forgotten who you are. This is a harsh truth but it happens.

Remember if you go to two meetings a week you will be having at least three one-to-one discussions and exchange of cards. After a month that is 24 business cards on your desk. After four months it is nigh on a hundred.

Trust me when I say it can all become a bit of a blur as to who was what and where you met them. However, when I am going through my amassed business card collection the people who jump most readily to mind are those whose face I can see.

So my advice is, if you want to be remembered have a good quality photograph taken and have it on your business card.

Here's another controversial statement:

I need to discuss your backside!

Should you print on both sides of the card?

I would say a firm yes to this. If your card is only one sided you are literally throwing away 50% of your advertising space. You are leaving blank a space that you could use to further inform your would-be client/new networking acquaintance of the services you provide.

The more people know about what you do the better they are informed to go out and talk about you when an opportunity arises.

It does mean that your card will be a bit more expensive to design and print but it will be of more use to you and to those you give it to plus it just looks more professional.

So now you've got your card, what do you do with it? Here is a great piece of advice I was given by a networker.

Wherever you are, whatever you are doing ALWAYS carry your business card with you.

Yes, all right, maybe not in the swimming pool but you know what I mean.

There is nothing more frustrating than to reach for your business card and not have one on you. It's happened to me a few times and the words of my friend start ringing in my ears. You just don't know when a situation may arise where it is appropriate to give your card to someone with a view to making contact at another time.

It is worth remembering that every social situation is an opportunity to network so take a few cards along with you should it be a school fete, the party of a friend or a night down the pub.

I blush at the thought of this but I attended the funeral of a distant relative and at the reception after a few drinks had been taken I got chatting to somebody who asked what I did and after a fairly detailed discussion he asked me for my card. I patted my jacket pocket and lo and behold my trusty cardholder was there and I was able to furnish him with a card and a couple of months later some work came from it. It just goes to show you should carry your card with you at all times 'cos you never know.... (by the way, Rest In Peace Great Uncle Morris).

A little tip that is obvious but not commonly acted on:

Keep your card in a little card carrier

I was on a commercial shoot recently and got chatting with one of the other actors who also worked as a copywriter for people's websites. It occurred to me that I might be able to pass his details on to this chap I knew (through networking) who was struggling with organising his website content so I asked him for his business card.

To say he was taken aback is something of an understatement. He grabbed his bag and started to rummage through it until he produced a bundle of cards that was bound by a rubber band. He handed me a dog-eared and rather ragged card with an apologetic smile mumbling something about how it was about time he got some more done.

The card itself was quite a good looking affair, but it was given to me in such poor condition that any credence the guy had built up in our conversation was destroyed the second he put it in my hand. Had the card been kept in a cardholder it would have been handed over to me in near pristine condition and I would have done as I said I would do and pass on his details to my friend. As it was I just thought that the guy didn't take himself seriously as a copywriter and by the look of things didn't actually do that much of it. All that deduced by the state of his business card. I graciously took his card but decided against contacting my friend.

A cardholder costs about seven quid. Not a lot to spend when you consider the cost of designing and producing your card in the first place. A small amount of money well spent.

Business card etiquette

There is, in my humble opinion, an awful lot of guff espoused from various quarters about so called 'business card etiquette'.

For example, I saw an online video presented by an American lady who talked about how she went to an all day networking event and chose to go with only three business cards so that she would be really judicious in who she chose to give them to.

She argued that this strategy stopped her from handing out her card willy-nilly to anybody with whom she happened to fall into conversation and prevented her from leaving with a clutch of business cards given to her by people she had no intention of contacting. She went on to say that if you are hyper-selective about who you talk to in the first place you will only exchange cards with whom you have struck a real and meaningful rapport. Eager to learn from the experiences of others I tried this. It doesn't work. Not in the UK at least.

Imagine you turn up to a meeting with three cards. You give them out. Then, all of a sudden, you are introduced to somebody who has a friend who would really benefit from the service you provide. They ask for your card and you shamefacedly have to say you don't have one left! In an attempt to rescue the situation you quote from some obscure YouTube video that gave you bad advice which you chose to take. Been there, done that and, thank you American lady, won't be doing it again.

I know Martin Gladdish holds a different view but in my opinion it really is as simple as this, if somebody offers you their card it would be deemed as impolite not to reciprocate by giving them yours in return. Furthermore, your business card isn't doing you any favours languishing in your wallet or purse.

Give it to someone who has had the decency to ask for it. It costs you practically nothing and in so doing you have cast a small pebble into the pool. Nothing may come back from it but in time something might.

Going in the opposite direction from our American friend I met this fantastic bloke who ran his own private detective agency called Ebony Services. Needless to say he is quite a character, full of jaw-dropping stories and fascinating titbits from the underworld of debt collection, fraud and infidelity. (I met him networking by the way – I wasn't under surveillance on this occasion).

He is always coming up with very astute ways of bringing his company to the attention of others. He decided to have a thousand cards printed and for two weeks he left them on trains, buses, in the back of taxis and minicabs.

He put a few on the bar of pubs, put a handful on the tables in the waiting rooms of doctors and dentists. Basically anywhere he went he left a trail of cheaply produced business cards in his wake.

On them he had no company name, no logo, no web address, or any other adornment such as lamination or colour printing. All he had on the card were seven words and his phone number.

'I promise I can help you. Call 07522 848843'

How clever is that?! It is witty, audacious, simple, caring and sincere all at the same time and above all it is engaging.

I put it to him that, while it's a fun wheeze, it was a mightily hefty claim and good as he was as a P.I. he might not have a Christlike touch whereby he could sort out absolutely everybody's problems. "I can't," he said, "but the likelihood is that I know somebody who can, even if I have to refer people to The Samaritans or social services or a decent shrink but in the meantime I've made contact with someone who has found out what I do, while pointing them in the direction of a solution."

He reckoned he spent thirty quid on the cards and had a return on his investment of 1000%.

That is a strategy that might not be right for every type of business but it just goes to show that being more generous in the way you give out your card can bring in big rewards.

How to avoid a stack of business cards the size of the Leaning Tower of Pisa

Believe me, it won't take long before you have business cards cascading out of every orifice of your suit and compartment of your briefcase. They seem to multiply like rabbits. You have to take control of this lest you get completely overwhelmed by the damn things.

I always log the information onto my Mailchimp account and hook up with my new acquaintances on LinkedIn and Twitter. In this way I know that I have their contacts details in a place where I can quickly get to them. Then I take the card and put it in a business card folder. I promise you will be amazed at how quickly it will fill up.

Once every three months or so I have a cull and let go of people's cards where there was no deepening of relationships. You will not – even if you wanted to – be able to have long lasting relationships of mutual benefit with everybody you meet so having a judicious clear out every now and again is valid and sensible.

And all of the above are a great illustration of why your card should be as well thought out and produced as possible – because your business card will be just one competing for attention among hundreds so....

Get it right and get it out there!

Chapter 12

Meaning and value of help

There are many out there who think that to ask for help weakens you and lowers other people's opinion of you. I cannot stress strongly enough how wrong this is.

If you are one of those who steadfastly refuse to ask for help for fear of somehow being viewed as a failure I tell you now, you are labouring under a misapprehension and missing out on a vital way of enhancing your networking experience.

Yes, it's true, the hard-hearted or mean spirited may sneer, but most people will come running to your aid without question.

At one time or another we all need and ask for help, but far from diminishing you in the eyes of those you turn to it actually humanises you. Yes we are showing our vulnerability but so what? As sole traders we are all vulnerable but as networkers we become one of a huge band of people who can aid, assist and help each other to move forward.

Why should you help people you hardly know?

In the first instance, believe it or not, helping others is a great way to fend off the blues.

When we help people our body releases a hormone called Oxytocin that not only induces feelings of warmth and euphoria but also a connection to others and as networking is all about cultivating those connections you can fast track the whole process by choosing to help those around you. It really is a win-win situation. Furthermore, by helping others you will live longer!

Research suggests that helping others may improve physical health and longevity as it actually decreases stress levels. It's an amazing thought that the simple act of helping somebody will lower your blood pressure and give you more time on the clock!

If that isn't enough to encourage you to help those around you, try this for an incentive. When you help, you're more likely to get help back. Several studies have suggested that your generosity is likely to be rewarded by others down the line – sometimes by the person you helped, sometimes by someone else. Also these exchanges promote a sense of trust and co-operation that will strengthen your ties to others. As well as all that you will be doing your reputation a power of good as a kind and helpful person on the network scene and people will be drawn to you.

Finally, when you give someone your help you will elicit feelings of gratitude and researchers found that gratitude is integral to happiness, health, and social bonds. So...

Help yourself by helping others

Having established that giving help is a key ingredient to being an effective networker, it is also good to know that if we ask for help we are almost guaranteed to get it because our brains are hardwired to help others. It's all down to the primeval need to keep the human race moving forward and progressing. Basically when we help each other we are more likely to survive as a species and this has a great pertinence for you as a networker.

Remember my first 60 second pitch when I said, 'I've come here today to ask for your help. I have no clue as to how to market myself so if there is anyone here who would be happy to offer me any guidance I'd be most grateful'.

Instantly an independent marketing consultant called Kirsty Egan-Carter introduced herself to me. We arranged a one-to-one meeting where she looked over my website, talked me through how to optimise it, showed me how to use my email as a way to advertise, discussed the value of LinkedIn and why it was a must for me. In later meetings she monitored my progress and offered accountability to help motivate me to action. All that help was given freely and without expectation of any return favour.

I did of course return the favour, how could I not? Kirsty had been so generous with her time and expertise that when she called me to say she had an important pitch to secure a long-term contract I leapt to her aid. I set aside as much time as was needed to give her one-to-one coaching on her presentation. Her pitch went well and she won the contract.

Since that time we have become solid friends and often meet for a catch-up. We pick each other's brains and when appropriate offer advice and support. An ongoing relationship of mutual benefit has developed and all because I asked for help.

My own experience with Kirsty supports all the studies and scientific research that I quoted at the top of this chapter.

Have a look at this list.

How I helped others:
- Filmed, and published about ten online videos for separate SMEs free of charge
- Recorded a series of five podcasts for an NLP practitioner to enhance her website
- Gave innumerable lifts to and from networking meetings
- Gave two seats per presentation skills workshop (numbering about 12 places in all)
- Supplied 'in the moment' coaching to anyone who asked for it
- Gave about 15 free personal impact coaching sessions

How others helped me:

- Received free design on my business cards
- Received free ongoing website support
- Attended a goal-setting course for free
- Became product ambassador for William Young 1876 Bespoke Tailors

- Received three professional photo shoots for profile pictures and website
- Shot four high quality online videos
- Received free design on my workshop flyers
- Innumerable lifts to and from networking meetings
- Recorded voice over audition CD
- Had this book proofread and retyped by expert personal assistant (thanks Heather)

There it is in black and white. If you help others you will receive the help of others in return.

Whilst putting myself out there for other people I was continually deepening my relationship with those I helped and the ripples of goodwill and reciprocated kindness came flooding back to me.
The minute you reach out to someone you feel a greater sense of connection to that person and not just one act of kindness comes back but two or three.

I met a guy at a BNI meeting who had recently turned his back on the corporate sector and he made a highly insightful remark about how the networking world in general is a far more compassionate environment to be in.

He said: "The corporate culture has a tendency to be more fearful and cut-throat. It's like if you help someone you are giving away your power whereas I think the more you help people the more you feel empowered and in the SME world there seems to be an unspoken understanding of this."

I promise you that within a week or two of continued and regular networking you will feel this generosity of spirit and you will be nourished, nurtured and encouraged by it.

Part Three:

Networking online – networking in life

Chapter 13

What is the best networking group for you?

There are basically three types of groups out there. Well, four if you include The Illuminate - a secret organisation whose membership is rumoured to include leading industrialists and ex-Presidents and Prime ministers. They are alleged to control world affairs by planting agents in governments and corporations to gain political power and establish a new world order.

Now if your master plan is world domination you should try and seek membership but as a sole trader I would suggest starting a bit further down the food chain before you try and hunker down with those boys. If you are happy to set your sights a little lower you might want to consider visiting or joining some of these:

National networking groups
Non-subscription groups
Independent groups

I think it's worth saying that all these types of networking groups have their own place and value. Some you will like, some you won't, but my advice is try them all and pretty soon you will end up focusing your attention on the groups that fit best for you. Let's break down the above list and explore the merits of each of its component parts.

National networking groups

Business Network International vs 4Networking

You've got a choice of two national subscription-based networking groups in this country. They are both very similar in their objectives and poles apart in their approach. Let's take a little time to compare and contrast.

Business Network International

Without doubt the largest networking group currently operating in this country, in fact the world, is Business Network International more commonly referred to as BNI. The group was founded in 1985 by Dr Ivan Misner, who said of his organisation, 'It is for the primary purpose of building powerful referral networks'. It seems to have done the trick. In less than 30 years it has grown exponentially from one little weekly meeting to where it is today – the behemoth of all networking groups.

This is the grand daddy of them all and some of their statistics make for very persuasive reading. Business Network International has operations in 45 countries worldwide with over 170,000 members. They have over 6,866 chapters covering the globe and for the year 2014 they claim to have facilitated referrals worth over £5.9 BILLION!

What are the rules?

Of all the networking groups I talk about in this chapter, BNI has the most stringent set of requirements for membership (and indeed continued membership).

- Each chapter allows only one person per occupational classification, and prospective members must be approved via an application process.

- BNI's philosophy is 'Givers Gain' - members are expected to focus on giving referrals to other members to build relationships and receive referrals in return.

- BNI draws a distinction between a ''referral' and a 'lead.' A lead is contact information for a prospect for a member's business, while a referral occurs only when the prospect has already expressed interest in the business in question, and is ready to be contacted by the referred BNI member.

- Chapters have specific rules regarding required attendance in order to cultivate the relationships needed to create a comfort level in referring business.

- Chapters track the monetary amount of passed business in order to prove the value of the financial and time commitment.

All that lot should leave you in no doubt that these guys mean business but what are the pros and cons to joining this group?

The pros

There is something very refreshing about the honest way in which they state that their aim is to help their members make money. Indeed, when you go to a meeting a certain proportion of time is always set aside to explain to visitors the potential earning capabilities of those people in the room.

They work out their annual chapter referral value and spread that across the chapter membership to give you the sometimes mind-boggling conclusion that 'a seat' is worth on average, let's say, £35,000 (This figure will change from chapter to chapter but I have certainly heard groups claim a seat to be worth this amount). It's mouth-watering stuff.

BNI meetings are held weekly and start early and I mean EARLY! The reasoning behind this is so that you can attend your network meeting and still have a full working day ahead of you.

One element of BNI that I think is excellent is the fact that it provides developmental training for its membership. They cover such subjects as referral generation as well as a rudimentary coaching in how to deliver a good 60 second pitch. They actively encourage their members to have one-to-one meetings with each other outside the chapter meeting to strengthen and enhance their understanding of each other's businesses and here's the big one: at each meeting referrals are handed out from one member to another there and then. You can actually see business being done right before your very eyes.

The cons

Some people may find the membership fee a bit high. Members have to pay a one off joining fee, an annual membership fee and a weekly meeting fee to cover room hire and refreshments. All in all you can expect to say goodbye to about £1,050.00 per year. However, any committed member will immediately point out that the benefits hugely outweigh the cost plus the outlay is spread throughout the year so it isn't too painful.

This whole issue of 'early and I mean EARLY starts'. The majority of meetings begin at 7am. Add the suggested arrival time of 6.45am to do some informal networking before the meeting proper and you are suddenly looking at getting out of bed often before dawn has actually cracked!

The structure and delivery of each chapter meeting can be a bit too transatlantic for some people's taste. There are initiation ceremonies where new members swear an oath with their hand placed on the BNI policy book and members are encouraged/instructed to applaud (a round of applause when a member hands over three referrals, a standing ovation for five).

I have to say none of this bothers me. It may feel a little manufactured at times but it is a great way to create a positive energy in the room and, just as with my wingman, a big celebration for a small win acts as great encouragement.

BNI expect a very high level of commitment. They make no apology for this arguing that for the group to be properly cohesive regular weekly attendance is vital. On the odd occasion when you can't make it you can bring in a substitute but if this happens too often your membership will be rescinded.

One big criticism that is often levelled at BNI is that it is a networking organisation where the biggest beneficiaries of all those riches spoken about previously are those who work in the trades.

Plumbers, electricians, decorators and builders certainly do well. A referral for those guys can be anything from a quick odd job to continued work on a building project where the value of the referral can go up into the thousands.

Having said that, I have been to many meetings where the membership includes long-term members from such varied professions as accountants, printers, executive car hire companies and solicitors all of whom swear by their BNI membership.

Strictly speaking you can only go to a BNI meeting if an existing member invites you. Fear not, after a short time on the circuit you will meet many BNI members and they are always keen to recruit so an invitation to a meeting is never far away. Also you can go online and find out the nearest group to you and ask to go along, I guarantee they will be friendly and welcoming.

My advice is to go along and see how you feel about the group, how it works and how it would work for you.

Sometimes the venue will provide a full breakfast but if you are unlucky all you get is a bacon roll!

After the meeting visitors are invited into a breakout room where a BNI member or director will take you through the application process. The intensity of this part of the morning varies wildly from a gentle chat where you are guided through the membership form and left to make a decision to sometimes (sorry to have to say this chaps) being a bit of an exercise in how to handle hard sell.

My view?

I really like BNI. The members are committed to their chapter and each other. It falls down for me only because, as an actor I might be dragged away for three months at a time and my continuity of attendance could not be guaranteed.

I have met many really great BNI members and I always go along to a meeting when I am invited. I find the members open and friendly and I have had members come along to my presentation skills workshops and recommend other friends of theirs to come along too.

As a networker, not to go along to a BNI meeting to try it out would be a mistake. They have a lot to offer, they are focused and professional. It isn't to everybody's taste but you won't know how it suits you unless you give it a go.

On a few occasions when I have been invited along as a guest to a BNI chapter I have had the pleasure to meet David O'Dell. He is the National Field Manager for BNI UK and a thoroughly decent chap all together. In the world of BNI he is a real heavy hitter so I am very lucky and extremely grateful for David taking the time to make a contribution to my book to describe what he thinks makes BNI different from its competitors.

Ladies and gentlemen, Mr David O'Dell...

Hi I'm David and having been a BNI member for eight years I am now the National Field Manager for UK & Ireland, my thanks in advance for reading my stuff about BNI as follows…

So, to start with, please let me ask you a question 'Why do you go networking?' – quite a big question eh? Maybe you are doing it without really thinking why?

I wonder, what is your networking goal?

- To have fun?
- To raid the buffet?
- To enjoy it?
- To make money?

Well, all of the above are good things, but at BNI we are focussed on the latter (although the other options are great as well).

When I started networking in the 1990s, I'd go for any of the reasons above. I'd heard that networking was the thing to do and so I went, I had fun, I definitely raided the buffet, sometimes stayed to hear the speaker, always thanked the host, usually enjoyed it, then made my apologies and off I went, with business cards stuffed in jacket pockets only to be retrieved when they went off to the dry-cleaners.

So in effect, my networking was a mile wide but an inch deep. I was too shallow. Then I decided, David, if you are serious about anything then you go for the serious option…

So let me ask you a second question – does JUST joining a gym get you fit? Of course not!

What do you have to do?

- Attend regularly
- Do what you are trained to do during the week
- Take advice and listen to your coach
- Be determined!

Once you are determined, you will become motivated and then see results...which using the analogy of a gym may be more energy, weight loss, getting fitter and feeling great!

Now I know there will there be days when you don't feel like going to the gym? Agreed...hmmm, yes, but if you want results...you will have to attend...

Imagine this, you turn up at the gym and you walk in to the foyer and it says bar, gym or jacuzzi – where will you go first? Well, I suppose it depends on why you joined! But if you want to get fit, then go to the gym first; then enjoy the jacuzzi and maybe the bar afterwards with no bad feelings. It's exactly the same in BNI – does JUST joining BNI make you £££? No, what do you have to do...

- Attend regularly
- Do what you are trained to do during the week
- Take advice and listen to your coach
- Be determined!

Because once you are determined, you will become motivated and then see results – which in BNI is making money.

So, in BNI we say let's 'get referral fit'...

Q. Why do we have name badges, membership ribbons, BNI pin badges and policies?

A. Because we are a serious business meeting and not a breakfast club...

Remember, serious business people who adopt our philosophy of GIVERS GAIN and want to network with other serious business people apply to join BNI as it is proven to make £££.

And finally, think about this, if you want to get fit, lose weight and be healthy, do you choose the cheapest gym and trainer who says turn up when you like? Or the one that will get you results if you apply yourself to the program?

If you want to network to make money and have some fun too, then I recommend BNI to you.

For more info, contact David O'Dell, National Field Manager BNI UK & Ireland - david@eurobni.com

4Networking

If BNI is the pin-striped suits and polished shoes of the networking world 4Networking (more commonly referred to as 4N) is the sports jacket and comfy shoes.

Founded in 2007 by man mountain and force of nature, Brad Burton the 4N philosophy is 'Meet, Like, Know, Trust' and to give you a taster of how they demonstrate this, one of their logos is a smiley face. When I first came across 4N I found it fascinating and hugely encouraging that it had built into its strap line the idea of chasing the relationship not the sale.

Overall I would say that 4N has a very user friendly feel to it and while the meetings are structured and always follow the same agenda the general feel in the room is much less formal than what you might expect to find at BNI.

What are the rules?

After you have paid your membership the rules are far more 'hang loose Mother Goose' than the BNI roster of requirements.

The basic rule is simple. For your passport membership (200 days for £200 plus VAT then £12 per meeting) you can go to any 4N meeting in the country up to five days a week. There, that was pretty straightforward wasn't it.

The pros

Annually, 4N hold more than 5,000 meetings throughout the year right across the UK. There's a 4N breakfast, lunch or evening group to choose from in pretty much every town and city in the country. This offers incredible flexibility for its membership.

If, like me, your work takes you all over the country there will likely as not be a 4N meeting you can attend should you wish to build contacts in that area.

For those of you who simply can't cope with the idea of getting up at 5.30am to attend your networking meeting, 4N start their meetings at a slightly more palatable 8am.

At each meeting you will arrange three one-to-one meetings with other members who you feel you might chime with. What is great about this is that you are forced to practice talking about your own business. Pretty soon any hint of WordBlur will go out of the window with the simple repetition of being in a protected environment where talking and listening is encouraged.

On top of the one to ones, should you choose, you can put yourself forward to give what they rather wittily call a 4Sight.

A 4Sight is an insight (get it?) on any subject a member may wish to talk about. It is not a sales pitch but more a speech to share useful information or give people another view of one's business. Occasionally you get a duff one, but for the greatest majority of the time people's 4sights are extremely engaging and there is always value in what is being presented.

Twenty minutes is allotted for the 4sight slot and at the end of each 4sight time is set aside for questions. The great thing about this is that for those few minutes everybody in the room is engaged in the same discussion, which I have always found a very unifying experience. For anybody who wants to go into public speaking the 4sight provides you with a great forum to practice your technique and any new content you want to try out.

4N has a brilliant online forum to help you continue your networking when you are out of the meetings. You get your own profile page and from there you can join in discussions, keep abreast with industry news, do some straight advertising or just have a gossip. If you want to you can publish an article with back links to your website to help your Google rankings.

The greatest thing about the forum though is how it acts like a LinkedIn for 4N members and because of the open nature of the organisation people are always up for listening online and being as much help as they can.

For your £12 meeting fee you get a fantastic breakfast – every time. Brad Burton is very much a man of the people and I suspect (though this is only a guess) the idea of going to work on a good breakfast is a directive from up on high from the big man himself (that's Brad, not God).

The cons

With a start time of 8am 4N meeting finishes at 10am. Once you've journeyed back home the best part of your morning is gone. For those of you who strive for greater time efficiency this might be worth bearing in mind.

Because your passport membership gives you access to every one of the meetings available you might be in danger of spreading yourself too thin and in so doing not coming across the same people as often as you'd like.

Remember, the best way to make networking work is to cultivate your relationships.

I would suggest concentrating your 4N efforts in a 35 mile radius. In this way you will never have to travel too far and you will definitely start seeing a broad range of interesting and helpful people who you will get to 'meet, know, like, and trust'. Pretty soon you will always know a few people at any 4N meeting you attend.

The two broad criticisms I hear about 4N are: 'None of their members have got any money,' and 'no-one is doing any business.' Not true. People invest money in their membership and if there were no return on investment those same people would very quickly stop coming and 4N would collapse like a pack of cards.

It's time for me to nail my colours to the mast here and say that I am and have been a member of 4N for the last two years. Not only have I enjoyed the more softly-softly approach to networking but I have spent about £3,000 on products and services of fellow members and reaped significant financial reward from the connections I have made there - not from the members themselves but who they were able to introduce me to.

I think there are many people for whom 4N didn't work and they moved to another networking forum – fair enough. Again, it's important to say that there is value in all networking groups but you need to road test them and see which one will best suit your personality and temperament. 4N suits me and I will happily continue with my membership for the long and foreseeable future.

My view?

Having already pointed up the fact that I am an enthusiastic member of 4N my view is probably a foregone conclusion. Guess what? I really like 4N. The people are genuine and helpful and after a short time my membership began to translate into warm leads and eventual business. In their bumf 4N describe themselves as 50% social 50% business. I think that is a clear indication of what to expect when you attend a meeting. Also it is a really hands-on organisation.

When I first joined I had a look at the online forum and saw that the founder of 4N, Brad Burton had posted something.

I decided to send him a quick message to say how much I was enjoying his audio book, 'Get Off Your Arse'. It was witty, insightful and, in my view, provided an extremely refreshing approach to helping business start-ups get going. Amazingly, 20 minutes later, he gave me a call. Yes, Brad Burton, multi-millionaire founder of the biggest joined up networking organisation in the country was calling little old me! Talk about personal service!

He asked me all about my business and then gave me the best bit of business advice I have yet to receive. "Paul, if you are as good as you think you are, get out there and organise some workshops at low cost so that people would be stupid not to attend. Build your reputation, sharpen your skills and then let those who came along act as your marketing team. If you're any good you'll get great word of mouth and things will start coming back to you."

I came off the phone and immediately put Brad's advice into action and I haven't looked back since.

So 4N works for me. If you want to see if it works for you, to use Brad's vernacular, 'Suck it and see!' Better still let's hear from the great man himself.

Ladies and gentlemen, Mr Brad Burton!

You run your own business. You need appointments. Right?
You started your own business because you wanted to work to your rules and timetable. Guess what? So did I.

And when I started 4Networking every other network in my view was too wishy-washy, or had outdated, daft rules and regulations that were created in the 80s and had not moved with the times.

In political terms, you had the Loony Left of networking, little or no structure, all very nice, lots people in a room, a bit like a school disco, but where nothing really quite happens. And then you had the Hardcore Right of networking, 'Where's your referrals?' 'Why didn't you attend the group last week?' 'You really need to bring more visitors ..'

I left full time employment to get off the hamster wheel and only narrowly avoided paying £500+ a year, to place myself back onto it again with my new boss being the networking group! I went along to one of these events; it was a bit like Scientology for business. No thank you. That wasn't for me, nor was it right for the many thousands of members who currently network with 4Networking. Look, I'm the founder of 4N; of course I'm going to be biased, but actually, I believe 4N is so great because it's different, it's a network and format that right at its heart, is a heart. 4Networking has a modern day culture and ethos of putting our members interests ahead of the organization.

Would you pass a lead, contact, refer business to someone you don't like, know or trust? Of course not!

So on that basis think about the reason people pass YOU leads, referrals and contacts, is it because they Like, Know and Trust you? Therein lies the core of what we do at 4Networking:

MEET - LIKE - KNOW - TRUST

Ironically, successful business networking is less to do with business and more do with people. If the buyer doesn't like the seller, it's going nowhere regardless of how great your product or service is. We are each deeper than the title on our business cards. Yes, it can take time to reveal those hidden depths and to build trust but I believe at 4Networking we have created the perfect environment to speed that process up.

At every meeting you get three 10 minute 1-2-1 meetings with people you choose. As well as having the choice of visiting ANY meeting of the 5,000+ we run each year across the UK in our joined-up network. Or connecting online 24/7 with 50,000+ online members, our members can build their profile and their confidence, find trusted suppliers, and become part of a supportive business community, all for less than £1 a day.

No other group can offer all this... It's a UK-born network for a UK audience. Effective networking needn't be hard work.

I think 4Networking is pretty unique not least because of the broad range of people who come along. We have members that range from a one-man band carpet cleaner to the MD of a £35m business. But remember at 4Networking it's not only the person you are talking with but all the people they know.

Ask the right questions, you'll get the right answers.

For relaxed, friendly and flexible networking – visit ANY of the 5,000 meetings we run each year in our UK-wide joined-up network. We built 4N into a truly national network, by throwing all the outdated policies of existing networks into the bin. We've made it a nice big UK-centric, national and friendly community.

I wouldn't have it any other way.

Choose and book a relaxed, fun and friendly 4Networking meeting near you at www.4networking.biz – you'll be made very welcome.

4Networking really is, business networking made easier.

Brad is never one to mince his words or sit on the fence about how he thinks good networking should be facilitated. In my view he has created something very special in 4N. Go and check it out and see what you think for yourself.

One last thing – 4N now has its own online TV Show. Look it up on YouTube, it's called 4NTV.

Chapter 14

What is the best networking group for you?
The Sequel

Non-subscription groups

Otherwise known as drop-in network groups these organisations are a fast and fresh way of getting some networking done. These meetings all have different scheduling. Some meet twice monthly, some have one meeting per month. Prices vary from about four to five pounds per meeting.

Perhaps the best known non-subscription network group was Business Biscotti. They recently introduced an annual subscription of £50 which is so low and is such good value for money I'm keeping them in this section. Biscotti have enjoyed rapid growth from their first meeting in 2007. Since that time it has expanded to 80 groups across 35 counties.

Another really happening drop-in group is Bizz Buzz, based in Hertfordshire to 'provide opportunities to meet, connect and share'. It started in 2008 and in 2013 it was awarded a Hertfordshire Business Award and is going from strength to strength.

These are just two examples of this type of group but there are many drop-in groups across the country. To find one near you just punch in 'local networking groups' plus your county into any search engine and there will be a comprehensive list for you to scan.

What are the rules?

You don't need to join, you don't need to book, you just need to turn up with your meeting fee and get networking. See what I mean about fast and fresh?

I asked Business Biscotti Ambassador Holger Garden to give me an overview of what their group has to offer.

"Business Biscotti is a business community that offers free informal networking, both online and offline. The community is nationwide with monthly meetings held at local venues that are convenient for people within regional branches of the community.

A monthly newsletter is sent to the circulation list of the local Biscotti club, as a reminder of the event. Meetings tend to attract more than 20 people whose interest is to network with other businesses in the area and identify opportunities for working together.

This is excellent value-for-money networking because once you've paid your £50 the only cost is for the refreshments at the venue."

The pros

If you prefer your networking on the hyper-informal side then these groups will suit you down to the ground as, at its core, you just turn up and talk.

Once you have attended one meeting they send you details of forthcoming meetings via email so you will always know where and when the next meeting will be.

The larger of these groups will have a membership arm where you pay an annual subscription that has more in common with BNI and 4N but there is no obligation to sign up.

All the same observations apply regarding the benefits of regular attendance and the futility of only making sporadic appearances but if you find a group you like and are prepared to commit to it this is networking at its least expensive.

If you want to set up your own group and reap the benefits of being at the centre of your networking activities, these groups make setting up a cinch.

The cons

The trade off you make for the laid back nature of such meetings is that you have to be prepared to get stuck in and talk and listen a lot!

There is no room for networking wallflowers here. Aside from a quick speech to welcome people there is no formal structure and you are quickly left to fend for yourself - for two hours!

There is no 60 second pitch. The opportunity to introduce yourself to all those attending is not on offer here. Again, you have to be prepared to approach people you don't know and network cold.

In their seminal book on networking 'And Death Came Third', Andy Lopata and Peter Roper highlighted the golden rule of networking as 'Chase the relationship not the sale'.

Well, at drop-in meetings you will see that rule being broken all around you. A lot of the people there will not be regular attendees or indeed experienced networkers so there is a high probability that you will come across those who are trying to make a quick sale in this environment.
The good thing about 'sellers' are that they are easy to spot so you can just extricate yourself but I fear you will need to extricate yourself quite often.

My view?

As a bolt on to my regular subscription-based networking, these type of meetings are great. Generally they tend to be very well attended and, for the most part, people are all there for the right reasons. I'll say it one more time – don't go once and expect to get anything out of it. Go regularly and often and in time you will see things coming back to you.

Independent Groups

These are small groups often made up of people who are in the same kind of business as each other. They act as a touchstone for those who want to keep their finger on the pulse of what is going on in their particular industry.

In a way they are like the old-fashioned guilds of the past. I have spoken at a few of these and their membership range from those in design, social media, business leadership and accountancy. You have to be invited to join this type of group. The membership is well priced and has a great deal of value for those who wish to keep themselves in the loop.

Another type of independent networking group is the privately run open to all type of affair that is currently proliferating countrywide. These tend to be really good fun largely because of the personalities of the people who run them.

A great way to network is to set up your own group. You act as a conduit for local businesses meeting each other, but at the same time get the real benefit of having all those disparate businesses meeting through you. Your contacts will be greatly enhanced and your profile at these meetings is the highest of anyone who attends.

There are a couple near to me that are worth a mention.

Local chap Nigel Oseland has set up something called 'BABs' where people rock up once a month at the end of the working week and network while sampling ale brewed on the premises of The Haresfoot Brewery in Berkhamsted.

As you might imagine, the atmosphere starts out as very relaxed and becomes more and more relaxed the longer you stay! It is a great place to do some laid back networking where everyone arrives with a mischievous smile on their face but with the serious intention of cultivating their connections at the same time.

I asked Nigel for a few thoughts on how he has benefitted from setting up his own group:

He said: "The idea was for local businesses to meet once per month in an informal setting with no agenda, elevator pitches or business card thrusting. We called our group BABS – Berkhamsted Afternoon Business Social. Our members offer a wide and interesting range of skill sets and like any good network a core group attended regularly and over time we built trust. We have not only done business together but have also become good friends."

Jonathan Reeves is the only accountant I know who ran his own pub (how's that for a USP?) During his time as the landlord of The Queen's Head Pub in Long Marston he set up a monthly networking group for people who lived out in the sticks.

With Jonathan at the helm as genial host it was a group that was welcoming, businesslike but homely all at the same time. I attended right up until Jonathan let go of his licence back in 2012. So missed was the occasion that he has set up another networking group in another pub and the good times continue to roll. Let's hear from Jonathan:

He said: "I needed to find an affordable way to create interest in my tax and accountancy business. I quickly discovered that adverts were high cost and low return. Eventually, I took the plunge and went nervously to my first networking meeting.

"Little did I know the very first person I spoke to would send me a lead to a remaining client – five years on. I was hooked straight away and I saw the opportunities and after a short period of helping to run events with others, I thought I can do this myself at the pub I owned so I created QH Networking that ran for two years.

"The great thing about running your own event is that everyone knows you and as a result they want to talk to you because you know everyone else, thus raising your profile, which is the key to networking. As my networking has grown so has my business'.

And how could I not include a comment from Vivianne Child, leader of Tring Together's BusinessMart.

"When, in 2008 we created Tring Together BusinessMart as a networking group, we were amazed at how wary people were of the word "networking'. We asked people who came to the first meeting what they wanted from a group and we got a lot of "well, what I DON'T want..." People had obviously had scary experiences in the past.

"We created a group that is exactly what those original members asked for; a warm and welcoming environment, provided by very friendly organisers, which encourages lively interactions among the participants. Therefore, regular as well as new members to the group instantly feel comfortable.

The aim of Tring Together BusinessMart is to instigate and maintain long lasting corporate relationships rather than the quick exchange of business cards. There are many benefits that are written on our application form; sharing knowledge with a wide variety of businesses, excellent presentations from guest speakers (including Paul Ryan!) on diverse business related subjects, etc.

However, it is the genuinely friendly nature of the group that encourages members to get to know each other, to trust each other and then to start to work together. At BusinessMart you don't have to pretend that everything in your business is perfect; we offer a safe environment to share concerns and problems with the group in order to receive strong support and valuable advice.

Tring offers a flourishing environment for local businesses to promote, network and benefit from each other. You are very welcome to join us, see www.tringtogether.org.uk for future dates.

Vivianne then went on to write this:

"Paul is a role model member of BusinessMart; consistently present despite his busy diary, consistently positive and consistently generous with his expertise."

If I'm being honest I nearly didn't include the last passage because, apart from making me blush I was worried that you, the reader might start thinking I was out to blow my own trumpet.

Then I realised that over and above the warmth and kindness of Vivianne's comment was an important bit of evidence that backs up my observations about going often to get the best out of networking, being open when you are there and being helpful and giving as a means to deepen you relationships – so I kept it in!

The pros

If you are looking for industry specific guidance and connections get yourself invited in to a group that is relevant to your strand of business. Anyone I have spoken to that is a member of such a group talks about how it is a more focused type of networking where people can talk in shorthand and keep up to date with current industry developments.

For the open to all networking groups the pros are simple. You will get an absolute up close and personal environment where you will be given an introduction by your host to anybody they feel will have a synergy to you.

The likelihood is that you will know the person running the event so it will feel more like a social gathering than the more classic networking occasion.

The biggest boon to this type of networking is that everyone attending will have their host as a common denominator and when people have faith in him/her they will have greater faith in those at the meeting thus connections tend to be enhanced more speedily and referrals and recommendations come about quicker.

The Cons

As long as you go regularly and often there are no cons. This is good, grassroots networking at its best.

So, you pay your money and you make your choice!

I hope you have found this breakdown of the different types of networking groups of use. It will give you a head start on what type of group you want to try first. My big tip though is to actually try them all. Remember, there is value in all of them but most value in the one you find that suits you. Happy hunting.

Chapter 15

Networking online – Twitter

Going back to my point that the greater numbers of people who go out into the networking field are 'of a certain age' and at a crossroads in their professional life, I am now going to make a sweeping generalisation. If this generalisation doesn't apply to you, well done, you can smugly read on knowing that you are in the exalted minority – or are you?

Here is the sweeping generalisation:

You hate social media, you don't see the point of it and can't see how it would be of any use to you or your business.

Be honest now, does this is include you?

Well, when I started Improve On You I wasn't exactly a social-mediaphobe per se, I did have a nodding acquaintance with Facebook but that was about it. However, I was shortly to have a baptism of fire.

When Kirsty Egan-Carter (my friendly neighbourhood marketing lady from chapter 12) sat me down to optimise my website, she asked why I didn't have any social media links. When I said I didn't do it, wasn't on anything and didn't see the point she gave me the sort of gentle smile a therapist gives to a deluded patient who thinks they are Jesus Christ - faintly intrigued but fully knowing I was in need of some serious help.

Kirsty patiently explained the benefits of three social media platforms, namely Facebook, Twitter and LinkedIn and gently nudged me out of my middle-aged intransigence into the brave new world of online networking.

Over a period of a couple of weeks she got me on my social media feet and set me off and running and I have to say the benefits are manifold.

So, if you are currently in the social media no man's land, have a read of the next chapter and get cracking. There really is no time like the present to put these things in place.

Social media will help you augment your in-life networking online and, conversely, help you to convert online introductions to in-life meetings that will further strengthen your opportunities to gain business through your network. And here's an interesting fact that will make you feel much better about the whole social media thing:

The fastest growing demographic on Twitter is the 55-64 year age bracket increasing 79% since 2012.

And here's another.......

The 45-54 year age group is the fastest growing on both Facebook and Google+

And another...

Two new members join LinkedIn every second.

This blows a hole in the notion that social media is just for the young and gives you a clue to the sort of reach an effective social media strategy could make available to you.

Let's start with Twitter.

Marian Murphy from Flourish with Social Media is an expert in helping businesses to grow through their online presence. She is also a Hootsuite certified professional and I am thrilled to say she has put together this guide to help you through setting up and getting started with Twitter as an effective networking tool.

Marian, over to you:

Using Twitter for networking
A quick overview

Twitter is a free social networking service that allows registered users to send out short updates of 140 characters in length called tweets. Twitter's own definition of its service says: 'Twitter helps you create and share ideas and information instantly, without barriers'. Twitter users can:

- Build up their own following of interested people and organisations

- Follow other Twitter users who could be individuals and/or representing a business

- Can see the tweets of the users they follow in their Twitter news stream

- Can retweet tweets (send tweets with content they like from those users they follow out to their own network of followers)

- Can mark as 'favourite', tweets from people or organisations they follow showing they like the content or to draw attention to themselves from that business

- Can use what is known as a hashtag, identified as #. A # is used to categorise your tweet on a particular topic. Any user can create a hashtag about anything and it brings together people who are talking about a certain event or topic.

- Some businesses use hashtags in their tweets to get noticed by people they want to attract.

- Can create Twitter lists - by using a list feature, a user can pull together the users they want to see content from the most or they can categorise the people they follow into different lists. Lists can be public or private.

There are a number of steps to follow to allow you to start networking on Twitter:

1. Set up your Twitter profile

First step to networking on Twitter is to set up a Twitter profile. You cannot follow updates from users of the service unless you are a registered user. To do this, go to www.twitter.com

You will then need to put in your full name, email address and password.

You must then decide on your user name/Twitter handle, which will look like this @yournamechoice. The total number of characters is 15 so ensure you have thought about this before you decide to set it up. There is also the possibility that your preferred username has already been taken, in which case you should have a back- up username.

If you decide at a later stage you would like to change your username, it is not a problem as long as it has not been taken by anyone else. Ensure your username is in line with your brand voice, message and company name.

2. Decide on a cover image for your Twitter profile

The header image is the large image for your Twitter profile. The recommended dimensions for this are 1,500 x 500 pixels.

Ideally this image should be in line with your brand voice and be consistent with your website and other social media imagery to give a unified message.

3. Decide on a profile image for your twitter profile

Your profile image is the small image on your profile and can be an image of yourself or your company logo. This will appear in every tweet you send out, so make sure it is professional, clear and in line with your business goals.

4. Make your bio count

Your bio is the area in your twitter profile where potential customers will see what your business is about. With a restriction of 160 characters, make these count. The essence of Twitter from its character restrictions on biographies and tweets is that it wants to keep the message simple. It is a great lesson in distilling what you have to offer and how you can be contacted.

5. Pin a tweet to the top of your profile

This is a very useful tool to use at varying times in your business, whether you have an event to promote, a book to launch, some free giveaway to capture your potential audience email addresses, a new product or an award you have received.

This will be the first tweet people see when they go onto your page so make it rock!

6. Tweet, Tweet!

Now you have the essentials nailed it is time to start tweeting. A statement I most frequently hear is 'I have nothing to talk about' or 'what can I say? Yes, it is scary if you have never been a business to talk about what goes on behind the scenes, in your industry or on general experiences during a typical day. I advise businesses to think about their content before tweeting and some general guidelines include:

- What services do you offer your customers? It is very interesting when I ask this, as many business owners stumble on verbalising what they do. If you are not clear, how can your target customers be?

- What human need do you satisfy for your customer? For example in the case of a hairdresser, instead of saying 'we cut hair', apply your service to your customer and convert 'we cut hair ' to 'we make our customers look amazing with our cutting edge hair designs'. So in a typical day a hairdresser can talk about what they have done with different clients' hairstyles and post before and after shots if the client agrees. This is then building up an image of the type of business in the minds of your potential customer.

- What are your hours of business? It may be different on different days so keep your audience informed regularly.

- Talk about the people behind the business   - let people see their personalities. For example, 'Julie is our amazing customer service champion. She will not rest until our customers are satisfied.' With this a photo of Julie could appear, showing the personality of the business and its professionalism.

- Talk about general topics that affect us all as human beings and that we can all relate to whether that is traffic, weather, food, holidays, birthdays, celebration days, inspiring quotations, great books, movies, TV shows to share with your audience.

- Create original or share curated content in line with your company product/service – so when someone decides to follow you they can see something of value and will be compelled to follow you because what you are saying is valuable too.

7. Netweeting! (Networking on Twitter)

Many businesses do not have a game plan when they decide to go on Twitter. They have seen other businesses talk about it and feel they should do it, but have not given any thought to why.

What is your business objective? Remember if you decide to manage your own Twitter profile, there is a commitment of time required, time which can often be spent doing other things. If you decide you will outsource/employ someone to manage your profile there is a financial cost.

You may have a number of business objectives:

- Increasing your brand awareness
- Building relationships with potential customers
- Increasing the amount of revenue from existing customers
- Promoting events or workshops you are running.
- Keeping your customers informed on operational news in your business
- Keeping new and existing customers updated on new products/services
- Using Twitter as a research tool to improve your product/service offering

Whatever your business objectives are, lay these out first and then decide who you want to follow. This will include existing clients, new target clients and influencers in your industry.

Think of who your business community includes; this may be local businesses and charities, local politicians and public figures, local councils, businesses you use yourself, suppliers to your business, or publications relevant to your industry who produce valuable content.

8. Targeting specific companies to network with on Twitter

Like any networking you need to decide the types of company you wish to target. Once you have identified the types of companies, locations etc, you can find out on their company website if they have a Twitter profile.

If they display the Twitter symbol on their website, click on this and this will take you to their profile.

When you get to their profile you can then start to follow them and their tweets. Once you start following your target companies, follow their updates closely.

You can then interact with their content in many different ways including replying to a tweet they send out, marking one of their tweets as a 'favourite' or retweet their tweets. These interactions all serve to flatter your prospective target and to make them take notice of you.

In time the hope is they will also follow you too and start to interact with your content. Once both users are following each other it is then possible to send a direct message to each other which is where you could send a link to some content you think may be of value to them, again building on the relationship.

It will make them feel special that you have gone to the trouble of sending them this information.

After a number of interactions and when you think the time is right, it may then be appropriate to ask who you need to speak to in the organisation or alternatively ask if you can pop in to see the person to learn more about their business and tell them about yours. That's Netweeting!

To find out more about Twitter and how Marian can help you go to: marian@flourishwithsocialmedia.co.uk
So there it is: a 1,500 word master class in all you need to know to get started on Twitter and cultivate one strand of your on-line networking arm.

I would just add that people love Twitter and devotees are often more reachable via Twitter than the more traditional routes of email or phone call.

A great example of how to benefit from keeping a relationship alive via Twitter is the fact that I got Canada's number one body language expert Mark Bowden to do the foreword for this book. We are old acting chums, but when Mark moved to Canada to start a new life, we kept in contact; first via Facebook but later through the odd tweet. It was via Twitter that Mark discovered that I was writing this book and offered to be a contributor. Hey presto! Netweeting works!!

Marion mentioned using hashtags (#). In Hertfordshire there is a great online forum that has been set up on Twitter called #Hertshour. It's a great way to get involved with local businesses and build awareness of your company. Anyone who is tweeting between 8-9pm on a Monday night using #Hertshour in their tweet is then part of a massive online chat. You can follow and be followed, find out what is happening in your local area, be seen and be heard.

There is also #Buckshour. Try putting in the hash tag and the name of your county and see what comes up. I tried a number of counties and they all had their own hash tag.

The other thing about Twitter is that a huge number of its users are accessible during their every waking hour! 25% of smartphone users aged between 18 and 44 say they can't remember the last time their smartphone wasn't next to them or on their person.

If the idea of Twitter still seems a pointless waste of time read this chapter again and then sign up. You will only benefit from doing this. There is certainly no downside to being on Twitter. Come on! Go into your stretch zone.

I know! Get yourself on Twitter and follow me. I'm @improveonyou. Even though I say so myself, I give great tweets full of free advice, links to my videos and the occasional podcast. Go on, you know you want to!

Chapter 16

Networking online - LinkedIn

LinkedIn is the social network for professionals. It continues to grow at a massive pace. Think about this; with two sign-ups per second that's more than 7,000 people and businesses per hour – globally. Not to get on board would be plain daft.

But ask yourself this: once on board do you take yourself on the LinkedIn journey or just sit in the station twiddling your thumbs?

A great deal of sole traders are on LinkedIn but do nothing with it. You really should. It will benefit your business and help you to network online before connecting in real life.

Angus Grady of CUSTOMEYES MEDIA is one of the country's leading LinkedIn experts. We met through networking a couple of years ago and Angus has agreed to give an insight into how to make LinkedIn work for your business as a key forum for networking online.

Get LinkedIn

There is a lovely Chinese word that describes the Chinese culture of building relationships ahead of doing business with a person.
That in a nutshell is exactly what LinkedIn is all about, a place to build relationships ahead of doing business, a place to build your brand value.

Guanxi is the word in question and is not a well-known word to many western business people, but it certainly reflects an oft-used maxim: Know, Like, Trust.

People buy from people and that will always be the case, if any of the three factors (Know, Like, Trust) are missing, then a meeting or sale is less likely to happen. I doubt if you would part with well-earned money on the basis of a quick meeting with someone you had never met before, if you had no social proof of what they did, or if they were not known to any of your network. Doubtless there are exceptions, but the basis of any transaction is trust.

How does LinkedIn work?

LinkedIn is a fantastic platform for developing that Know, Like and Trust and for building lasting business relationships. It is a networking platform that is perfectly designed to grow your connections online and do business with offline. There are no quick fixes. Trust takes time and the same rules apply online as offline. Have good manners, be generous, offer your help before being asked for your help and never, but never, over sell.

Building reputation and not trying to get a sale is often the objective and LinkedIn is perfect for this. It is far better to have a good reputation for delivering quality advice and information, than having one quick meeting in the hope that there could be a potential sale.

Like all good networking it is always about what you give, not about getting to the sale in the fastest time possible. LinkedIn helps to build those touch points and when you ask for a telephone meeting or suggest a face to face meeting then you are more likely to succeed.

The underlying paradox of the internet is that we are more connected than ever yet less connected...some boast of having thousands of connections but how many of those do they engage with?
By having a strategy and a plan it is very easy to nurture connections so that however big your network is you will always have a core of connections that are important to your business. A personal collection of business contacts that is easy to follow, message and introduce to others.

More than anything it lets you nurture warm business relationships online that help an offline meeting go well.

LinkedIn works on so many levels and it would be easy to go off on a tangent, but a quick overview is worth noting.

It's a collection of over 300 million people all of whom have personal profiles and company profiles that are searchable. It is a database of market intelligence, a publishing platform, a chat room and an index of business opportunities. It is recruitment, marketing sales and networking platform all rolled into one.

You can rekindle old contacts, look for new connections in your target market and form bonds with people in your market sector, carry out market research and find new niches.

Joining Groups and being part of discussions all help to make sure that your profile gets noticed, share updates, endorse and view profiles.

Referring and recommending people that you have worked with further builds business relationships and extends your reputation and expertise to people outside of your network.

The F Words

These are by no means what you might think, they are Find and Found.

A well written profile backed by activity (posts and joining in discussions) gets you noticed; people will ask to connect and meet with you as you are showing that you are an expert and willing to share advice and content. That's the Found side of things.

Find means that you can search for people that you want to be connected with, people in your target market or sector. Find key people in the exact business sectors that you want to do business with.

When you have a clear and precise target market mapped out then your LinkedIn research will deliver potential connections whose problems are directly solved by your business solutions.

How do you take the online offline?

Make sure that you are sharing valuable content in groups and in your updates and you will get noticed, you will attract connections with your expertise and willingness to help. You will be seen as the expert in your field and your opinion will be sought after.

Most of us will attend face-to-face networking groups already.

Connect with people that you are not already connected and start to build that trust. If you are part of a larger networking group, take the opportunity to contact people in a certain area and ask if they would like to meet after the event. It's an easy way to make sure that your time is well spent and to further cement business relationships with those you meet.

Join the Group on LinkedIn that your offline-networking group has and comment, help and contribute.

Research who attends each of the networking groups you go to and make sure that you have researched what they do and what they have shared. This gives you the chance to ask better questions and further build confidence and trust.

Publish on LinkedIn and ask questions of your readers and suggest connecting and sharing information. Networking reaps rewards for those that get involved, contribute and listen. LinkedIn is a great place to do that, but its true worth lies in being able to help make face to face networking work even better for a business.

Imagine knowing something about the other people in the networking group you attend? You can offer more help and make the face to face meeting that much more productive by having that deeper understanding of what they might need.

Networking in its true sense is a combination of online and offline, they are two sides of the 'Know, Like, Trust' coin. Offline I go to a various mix of business networking events. When networking online I use LinkedIn first and foremost because, for me, it yields the best results.

If you want to get more expert advice from Angus at CustomeyesMedia just punch in 'Angus Grady' on Google – he's top of the page.

All social media platforms change and evolve and one of the great things about the way that LinkedIn has moved forward is how it is now far more accessible via your smartphone. It has kind of morphed into a more user-friendly, less stuffy environment where, for example, people's birthdays are flagged up and you are notified when someone you are linked to is having a work anniversary. This may sound trivial but it offers you a great excuse to get in touch with somebody.

Some think the tool has been dumbed down as a result of these changes. That may be so, but for me it makes the whole user experience a better one. I recently pinged over a note to say happy birthday to someone who immediately got back in touch to say I was just the person she was after. Two weeks later I was leading a series of workshops on clear communication in the field of health and safety.

There are literally hundreds of social media platforms out there. Ignore them at your peril. It is difficult to know where to begin, I know, but just get started and pretty soon you'll get the hang of it and begin seeing the benefits of your hard work. From a business point of view, I think Twitter and LinkedIn are a great starting point.

You have the über chilled and swinging Twitter, which is potent but low stress and the other end of the spectrum with LinkedIn, the most business driven social media site. Somewhere in the middle of those pick another one and develop that too. Link them all to each other and in a short space of time you will have built an online foundation stone for your business that will aid and support all your other offline networking efforts.

So we have covered every available group type, a few of the online platforms and a number of offline opportunities that you can explore to build your network and make it as strong, effective and supportive as possible but there is one last place we need to talk about before we finish this final part of the book.

The Last Place To Network

Everywhere else you go, any time of day, any time of night where there are other people gathering together in a social context you will be networking.

Anything you want to achieve in your life will be through or with other people from all walks of life with different skill sets, interests and levels of ability. So use every day to increase your network.

Are you a keen reader? Join a book club and meet people.
You like mountain biking? Then find time to get out there and ride with others who share the same hobby.

Are you into a good pub quiz? Great, off to the boozer with you and sit among the local intelligencia knitting your brow over the multifarious conundrums set you by your pseudo-intellectual landlord.

Do these things because all the time that you are pursuing your interests with others they will be getting to know you, who you are, what you do and where you do it and thus your network will be ever growing.

This so called 'Passive Networking' is the final piece in the puzzle of where and how to network. Being social, being seen, being heard in this way will, one day, bring rewards when you least expect them.

Use all that you have learnt in this book about the formal business networking environment and apply it to your social life. Never sell, always listen, give of yourself with no expectation of getting anything in return and you will enjoy a rich collection of friends and a wide and stimulating set of life experiences while quietly building a network that will add even greater reach, strength and value to your formal networking activities.

Epilogue

Off you go!

That's it! Off you go! My work here is done!

If you use all the tips in this book:

- Make the effort to get out there and network on a regular basis
- Give help often and ask for help when you need it
- Remember the power of your own personality and experiences
- Know the difference between fear and 'fight or flight'
- Remember the 60 second ABC
- Utilise all the body language tips I mentioned to enhance your confidence levels when public speaking
- Don't go to sell
- Have a business card you are proud of
- Don't go to talk, go to listen
- Log business card info post meetings
- Organise out of meeting one to ones

...and choose a group that best suits you, then I have every confidence that you will not only gain great benefit from your networking activity but enjoy it as well.

The enjoyment element might sound like a trivial thing to pick up on as this book draws to a close but actually, it is one of the most important things you should be doing while you network. When we enjoy what we do we tend to do that thing more often and more thoroughly so make it more enjoyable by making friends out there! If you take on board all the advice about deepening your relationships, seeking out those with whom you have struck a rapport and building a closer acquaintance with them; pretty soon it won't feel like you're networking at all but socialising with a profitable business outcome.

You are now equipped with an understanding of what to expect when you step into the networking environment and how to best gain traction from your efforts. Yes, you will go through highs and lows, sometimes wondering if it is all worth the effort but I promise, if you stick with it, networking will be a powerful mechanism in helping you and your business move forward and flourish.

Before you go any further I want to end this book at the beginning of your life as a networker.

The beginning...

Now go get 'em!

No More Networking Nerves

If you enjoyed this book and would like to attend my No More Networking Nerves workshop to gain even more potent learning and expert tuition on your rapport building abilities and presentation skills go to my website at www.improveonyou.co.uk

To find out when the next event is being held or if you run a company and would like me to bring my workshop to you give me a call on 07973 241289.

I guarantee a hugely enjoyable learning experience. It's not just me who thinks I'm ace! Here are some testimonials from previous attendees:

'As an experienced public speaker I attended Paul's event with curiosity – but I was blown away – it was in turn inspiring, reassuring, thought provoking and often laugh-out-loud funny. But most importantly I saw nervous networkers transformed over a couple of hours in to losing their fear of speaking and networking.'
David O'Dell National Franchise Support Manager for BNI UK and Ireland

'Paul has a fantastic way of engaging a group of people who have never met. Not only will you come away with lots of confidence but you'll have had a really good laugh in the process as Paul is very funny. Totally worth it!'
Cheryl Burton, Senior Partner at Park Health and Safety

'I cannot recommend Paul highly enough. He is the ultimate professional making you feel at ease and enjoy the session so much that time just flows.'

Sue Prytherch, MD Natural Talents Executive Search

INDEX

D

David O'Dell   148

Dee Blick   7

Dr Ivan Misner   142

E

Eye contact   74

F

Fight or flight responses   49, 50, 51, 52, 64

Find and found   186

Following-up   87, 88, 93

G

Get off your arse   23

Guanxi   184

H

Help yourself by helping others   135

Henry Ford   104

J

Jeanette Lendon   7

Kirsty Egan-Carter   136, 172

L

LinkedIn   183

Listening   58

51532684R00111

Made in the USA
Charleston, SC
25 January 2016